DIVIDE

Albury

Lancefield

Newham

Kilmore

Romsey

DIVIDE

Mt. Macedon

Creek

Deep

Darraweit
Guim

Maribyrnong or Saltwater River

Riddell's Creek

Gisborne

Sunbury

Bulla

Melton

Kororoit

Tullamarine

Ck.

Keilor

Essendon

River Yarra

MELBOURNE

To Geelong

River

Port Phillip Bay

The Crisis in Victorian Politics

1879-1881

Alfred Deakin, about 1880

The Crisis in
Victorian Politics, 1879-1881

A PERSONAL RETROSPECT

Alfred Deakin

EDITED BY

J. A. LA NAUZE

Ernest Scott Professor of History, University of Melbourne

AND

R. M. CRAWFORD

Professor of History, University of Melbourne

MELBOURNE UNIVERSITY PRESS

First published 1957

Printed and bound by Halstead Press, Sydney
for Melbourne University Press, Carlton, N.3, Victoria

Registered in Australia for transmission
by post as a book

London and New York: Cambridge University Press

Dedicated
by the editors to
HERBERT BROOKES
who has cherished and
added to the Deakin papers
so that Australians may
come to know one of
their founders

CONTENTS

Introduction   xi

1 'Whirled into Politics'
   The West Bourke Candidature, 1879

2 'Power Actually Despotic'   11
   Graham Berry and his Government, 1877-9

3 'Gay Irresponsibility'   24
   The Election for West Bourke, 1879

4 'The Absolutely Unexpected Climax'   35
   Resignation, 1879

5 'Election Pranks'   44
   Episodes in Campaigning, 1879

6 'Beginning to be Sobered'   52
   Defeat and Victory, 1880

7 'A Course of My Own'   62
   The Reform Bill, 1880-1

8 'Leaders at a Bound'   71
   The Passing of the Reform Bill, 1881

Appendix A. Persons Mentioned in the Text   82

Appendix B. Deakin's First Election Address   87

Appendix C. Victorian Ministries, 1877-83   89

Index   93

ILLUSTRATIONS

Alfred Deakin, about 1880   *frontispiece*
  By courtesy of Lady Rivett

Sir Graham Berry   *facing* 16
  By courtesy of the Public Library of Victoria

Election Handbills, 1879   28, 29
  By courtesy of Lady Rivett

'The Berry-Blight on the Ballot-Box'   *facing* 32
  Reproduced from Melbourne 'Punch', 1879

Sir John O'Shanassy   *facing* 64
  By courtesy of the Public Library of Victoria

The West Bourke Electorate, 1879   *end-papers*

INTRODUCTION

IN THE LATER MONTHS OF THE YEAR 1900 Alfred Deakin wrote two
memoirs of that phase of Australian history, and of his own life
as a statesman, which the coming proclamation of the Commonwealth of Australia would shortly bring to an end. The first, cover-
ing 1898-1900, completed his account of the Federation movement,
in the final episode of which he had so recently been engaged as
one of the delegation sent to London to watch the passage of the
Enabling Bill through the Imperial Parliament. The complete account,
edited by Deakin's son-in-law, Herbert Brookes, was published in
1944 as *The Federal Story*.[1] It is a vivid recollection of events still very
recent to Deakin as he wrote about them. In the second memoir he
went back twenty years to the beginning of his political life in Victoria. Whereas his account of the Federal movement had almost
entirely omitted references to his own activities, the present memoir
is a chapter of autobiography, as well as an historical essay 'for the
information of those curious as to the real manner of conducting the
affairs of a colony prior to the Federal Union'. Walter Murdoch
printed some passages from it in his *Alfred Deakin—A Sketch*
(1923), and in the text of his early chapters followed Deakin closely
in a number of places. In her unpublished thesis, 'The Economic and
Political Development of Victoria, 1877-1881' (1951),[2] Dr J. E. Parnaby also quoted passages from the manuscript to which she had been
given access. The full and continuous narrative is now made available
for the first time. Deakin had intended his account of political life
in Victoria to cover his experiences from 1878-1900. When it was 'put
aside December 1900 incomplete' (a few days after he had declined
the offer of a Privy Councillorship), he had in fact covered only
the first four years of that period. Within a month he had assumed
office as the first Attorney-General of the Commonwealth, and in
the next decade was to be three times Prime Minister. It is therefore
likely enough that the memoir would in any case have remained
incomplete. The reason for suspending it on 4 December 1900 can,
however, be precisely given. Deakin had just received from London

---

[1] Robertson and Mullens, Melbourne, 1944.
[2] Deposited in the Melbourne University Library.

the cable which was the signal to begin the weekly articles on Australian affairs which he was to continue to send to the *Morning Post* until 1914. In fact he posted his second article on 5 December, and was therefore almost certainly writing it on the very evening that he added and signed the hasty postscript to what was to remain the final chapter of his Victorian memoirs. The curious story of the *Morning Post* articles has been told elsewhere.[3] They too were to be deliberately written as materials for historians in the future. The leisure either to resume the memoirs of 1900, or to write the short history of the Commonwealth in its formative years which he later contemplated, did not come until 1913. Then it came only to find him recording in agonized passages the stages in the disintegration of his shattered memory.

Although these chapters cover only the first few of his twenty years in Victorian politics they have an historical and autobiographical unity. They deal with a short and distinct period of intense political passion in the life of colonial Victoria, still instructive to the student of democratic institutions; a period appropriately concluded with the passing of the Reform Bill of 1881. Deakin himself, an unknown youth in 1878, had in that time risen with extraordinary rapidity to a position of high political prominence. There was a certain artistic fitness in his leaving the narrative unfinished at that particular point.

Deakin's brilliant gifts as a narrator are illustrated here, as in *The Federal Story*. But his memoir is not only a vivid and sometimes dramatic narrative. Despite the fact that it is entertaining to read, it is an historical document of some importance. Deakin himself is well aware of the limitations of personal recollections as materials for the historian; but they are a necessary part of those materials. His narrative does not now add much that is new to the 'inner history' of the actual events of that time of crisis. Its importance lies rather in the point of view from which it is written. The more familiar accounts of these events, in particular those of G. W. Rusden in his *History of Australia* and Henry Gyles Turner in his *History of the Colony of Victoria*, are strongly, indeed ludicrously, biased on the 'Conservative' side.[4] Deakin writes as an active participator on the

---

[3] See J. A. La Nauze, 'Alfred Deakin and the *Morning Post*', *Historical Studies— Australia and New Zealand*, vol. 6 (1955), pp. 361-75.

[4] G. W. Rusden, *History of Australia*, 3 vols (Melbourne, 1883, second edition 1897); H. G. Turner, *A History of the Colony of Victoria*, 2 vols (London, 1904).

'Liberal' side, a supporter and in many respects an admirer of Graham Berry, whom readers of Rusden and Turner would take to be no more than a dangerous and reckless charlatan. Some care is of course needed in the interpretation of the terms Conservative and Liberal. At the beginning of Chapter II Deakin explains very clearly what they could be generally taken to mean in the seventies and eighties; but though something like organized parties probably emerged earlier in Victoria than elsewhere in Australia, the labels should not be taken to imply a dichotomy as clear cut as their counterparts in Britain at that time, far less a distinction like that between labour and non-labour parties of a later generation. It happens indeed that the distinction, based very roughly on economic interests and status, was sharper in the years 1877-81 than it was to be later when coalition governments tended to soften the asperities of the Berry period.

After twenty years Deakin could view the events of that period with a good deal more calmness than Turner, whose book, published in 1904, was written at about the same time as his own memoir. Turner was still quivering with a personal loathing of the Liberals and their policies. Deakin could see faults and mistakes on his own side, but presents a view of the Conservatives which provides a more satisfying explanation of the antagonisms of the time than Turner's simple references to 'the mischievous pranks which [Berry] was encouraged by the masses to play with the well-being of his fellow-men'.

In another way Deakin more than fulfils his hope that his memoir might 'possibly hereafter have some interest to others'. Sometimes in a packed single sentence, sometimes in a formal set piece, he gives vivid descriptions of the appearance and personality of the men whose actions he is describing. No doubt there is an element of caricature in some of these, but they live. Acknowledged or not, they will be repeated by those who come to write about that generation. The set pieces on Berry or Pearson, for instance, are irresistibly tempting as quotations. So are the formal contrasts characteristic of Deakin's style, as when he writes of O'Loghlen and O'Shanassy: 'The genial, gentle, indolent, lethargic, procrastinating, improvident and impoverished Baronet was as manifestly his rival's superior by birth, breeding and education as he was his inferior in strength of will and character and intellect. Physically a giant with a splendid head and rugged features of proportionate dimensions, O'Shanassy was the peasant in build, gait and habit, though lifted by his life's training and brain-power as clear of his compatriots of the same class as was Burns by his genius.' So, one by one, does Deakin bring to life the men of the first generation after the gold-rushes, when the Australian society of today first begins to be recognizable.

After some consideration we decided to omit from the text, the original manuscript of which will in time be available to scholars, a few phrases and sentences referring to persons. These omissions are indicated in their place by the conventional dots. In view of Deakin's known practice in parliamentary controversy it seemed likely that if he had himself published the manuscript he would have deleted some more than usually harsh phrases. Further, we considered that while all persons referred to in the manuscript are dead, the deleted phrases, while not affecting the narrative in any essential way, could possibly have caused pain to living persons.

The original manuscript, written with rapid fluency on one side of the half-quarto sheets resembling 'copy paper' which recall Deakin's journalistic days, was never revised. Such alterations as there are in the text were clearly made in the process of composition. We have perforce largely supplied punctuation which, beyond dashes between sentences, hardly exists in the original. We have also made occasional editorial insertions of omitted words clearly required by the context, corrected occasional slips in the spelling of proper names, and so forth; we have not thought it necessary to draw attention to such incidental details but all editorial insertions of any consequence are enclosed in square brackets. The footnotes are entirely ours. They are intended merely to provide the minimum information necessary to elucidate references in the text to events which would have been more familiar to readers in 1900 than they are today. If some of these seem hardly necessary to those who know their Victorian history, it should be remembered that there are many who do not, but who are nevertheless interested in Deakin in a wider context.

Since some names recur at widely separated intervals, we decided to omit biographical footnotes and to bring together all general biographical information in an alphabetical list at the conclusion of Deakin's text.

We wish to emphasize that the manuscript is now published as an historical document, and that we have deliberately refrained from intruding our own assessments of the validity of Deakin's judgments of policies, persons, or events. In one instance (p. 18) where he is avowedly reporting a rumour, it seemed helpful to include a note of some length. Otherwise we have let his narrative stand without comment. Similarly we have not attempted to give references to accounts by later writers of the period discussed by Deakin. The most detailed of these is the thesis by Dr Parnaby which we have already mentioned.

We have been helped in various ways by Miss Margaret Kiddle, and by Mr P. Garrett and other members of the research staff of the Public Library of Victoria. Miss Joyce Wood drew the map of the West Bourke Electorate. We tender to them our best thanks.

J. A. LA NAUZE
R. M. CRAWFORD

'WHIRLED INTO POLITICS'

The West Bourke Candidature, 1879

THE CHAPTER OF MY POLITICAL LIFE in the Parliament of Victoria
now closing seems sufficiently interesting to me to indulge in a
retrospect which may possibly hereafter have some interest for
others.[1] The true perspective in politics in regard to any person is
hard to find and harder to keep. Current contemporaneous opinion
is extremely apt to err by being too partial and too short of span, while
the historian on the other hand is liable to be so well-informed, so
broad in outlook and so biassed by the actual trend of events as
known to him when looking backward, that scarcely a biographer
is sympathetic or free-minded enough to be accurately just. Those
who happen to have been on the winning side or what seems so at
the time of writing become glorified as heroes, while those who were
opposed or associated with other movements which have failed to
take root are—unless for the purposes of party—censured or passed
by upon the other side. But the volume which might be written
upon human misconceptions as illustrated in each generation either
by [its] misunderstand[ing of] itself [and] its predecessors, or
[by the way in which it is misunderstood by] its posterity is scarcely
worthy even of an outline,[2] so obvious is it to those who have mixed
with affairs that the whole truth of any situation would require a
library of biographies and histories written candidly from many
standpoints for its complete presentment; while the kaleidoscope

1 The Commonwealth of Australia Constitution Bill received Royal assent on 9 July
1900. Alfred Deakin reached Melbourne on 17 July on his return from London as a
member of the Australian delegation sent to watch the passage of the Bill through the
Imperial Parliament. On 22 September he publicly accepted a requisition to stand as
a Federal candidate for Ballarat. The Victorian Parliament was dissolved on 18 October,
and after twenty-two years Deakin was no longer a Member of the Legislative Assembly.
On 1 January 1901 he was sworn in as Attorney-General in the first Federal ministry.
At the first Federal elections, held on 29 March 1901, he was returned as Member for
Ballarat in the House of Representatives.
2 The syntax of the unrevised sentence in the original has gone astray, and the
probable meaning has been guessed.

of twenty years of life even in a colony surpasses all hope either of
achievement or of deserving to be achieved.

This is less regrettable because unless committed to paper day by
day in a continuous and ample record never afterwards tampered
with, the most conscientious writer of memoirs will find himself
insensibly shaping such material as his memory retains in the light
of his later judgment and experience, remembering only what throws
light upon what seem to him then matters of importance and ignor-
ing much which formerly disputed supremacy of his thoughts and
purposes. It does not follow, of course, that we see truly at any
moment. We may have been purblind from day to day; but whether
we are or are not any clearer sighted when we come to set down
our recollections, we can only give at best a rendering of facts as
they appeared or as we now think they appeared to us in former
times. These reflections may discourage one from writing at all, or
they may prompt the garrulous to put aside all pretence, and as they
must needs be limited to their own tale, determine to tell it frankly
and with that preliminary postulate give rein to egotism. Personal
they must be and personal therefore they had better openly begin and
remain.

My earliest political recollections are of hearing discussions of the
deadlock of 1865 and of engaging in school conflicts upon the Free
Trade versus Protection issue which was then dividing the country.[3]
My father was a Free Trader and that was of course enough for me,
as for my fellows, who no doubt were in the same utter ignorance
of the meaning of the battle cries we raised and of the cause for or
against which we fought. In this incident the philosophers might
perceive a forecast of much that continues to pass for politics with
the electors. A parable built upon these lines might be appropriately
introduced; but after all what could it [achieve] except dress up
the fact in eastern or other picturesque costume. As boys we dis-
dained argument and definition. All we needed was to know that
there were two parties engaged in strife, under certain shibboleths
which we could by repeating make occasion for conflict, not of the

---

[3] The deadlock between the two Houses of the Victorian Parliament. The Legislative Council in July 1865 refused to consider the Appropriation Bill, so long as a
Customs Bill was tacked to it. The struggle, ostensibly on a point of constitutional
principle, soon divided the colony into supporters of free trade or protection, and the
deadlock was not resolved until April 1866. Deakin was at the Melbourne Church of
England Grammar School, 1864-71.

serious kind to be settled by fists or duels of one to one, but by harmless missiles consisting of clods of earth, usually held together by tufts of grass, or of loose sand wrapped in paper and bursting like shells when they struck. With these primitive projectiles we gaily pursued each other in bands about the playground and hugely enjoyed our participation in the excitement of the hour. There were no turncoats, no leaders, no programmes, and no quarter asked or taken for the short time during which this pastime reigned. When it disappeared as suddenly as such novelties do in public schools it took with it the only political interest which I can remember to have been manifested by others, or to have existed in myself, during my school days.

My father read only the *Argus*[4] and like most men derived nearly all his opinions on current affairs from that journal, which naturally therefore spoke to me with double authority. So soon however as I began to read serious literature at all, at this time mainly poetry, I despised both the daily press and local politics, thus escaping the influence of both parent and paper. The towering figure of Higinbotham, in spite of partisan slanders, began to impress me, and the battle for the Education Act passed in 1872 made me for a time an ardent politician. Then the Stonewall episode[5] of 1875-6 attracted my attention to parliamentary proceedings; but this was merely as a spectator and it would soon have waned had not the candidature of Professor Pearson for the Assembly satisfied me that the Liberal Party in the colony was entitled to the sympathy of one who like myself was at that time saturated with the doctrines of Spencer, Mill, Buckle, superimposed upon an earlier and more durable foundation from Carlyle, Ruskin and Emerson. A philosophical radical as I should have styled myself, I had been repelled from Mr Berry and his supporters by the caricatures and calumnies of the *Argus*. If, however, a scholar and a gentleman, a historian and publicist like Pearson, was prepared to become their ally it was plain that I need have no hesitation in following the same flag. My first attempt

4 First issued under that name, 1846. Purchased by Edward Wilson 1847. During the nineteenth century the 'conservative' and free-trade journal of Victoria.

5 A debate in the Legislative Assembly, beginning on 8 February 1876, was continued without intermission until late on 10 February by the expedient of moving word-by-word amendments. The epithet 'Stonewall', after the Confederate General, applied to themselves by the Opposition (Graham Berry's followers) was apparently first used in this sense in connection with this and similar incidents (see *Oxford English Dictionary*, s.v. 'Stonewall').

to attend a public meeting was early in 1877 when he was contest-
ing Hawthorn against Mr Murray Smith, an almost impossible seat
for him to have challenged and to which he had been sent, no doubt,
by the advice of men who desired to make use of his inexperience
by setting him a task that no-one else was likely to face. Having
been misdirected I arrived late and was greatly disillusioned then to
find him speaking in the corner of a large room in an hotel crowded
with a working class audience tamely listening to a quiet and thoughtful address delivered like a lecture. I could only obtain standing room
in a draughty passage and left after a few moments without having
heard more than a few passages of his speech.

I had at this time no taste for local politics and no thought of ever
being concerned with them though I had enjoyed a fair amount of
speaking at the University Union, of which Professor Pearson was
for a time Chairman; at the Eclectic Association, a monthly Free
Thought meeting; and the Lyceum, a Sunday School conducted
chiefly by Spiritualists but under similar auspices. Many public questions were more or less debated at these gatherings, but mainly in
an abstract way and with little reference to practical politics. I was
still by inclination a student, reading hard and at large books,
pamphlets and magazines with a preference for those that were
literary, poetic, artistic or speculative. Of course the principles of
my favourite author Spencer were made mine; but I was in no way
eager to attempt to apply them to the colony in which I lived, of
whose extent and resources, people or their opinions, I knew as little
as was possible to one whose life had been passed within its bounds
and whose thoughts were everywhere or nowhere. On attaining
my majority I had seen but a few stray copies of the *Age*[6] whose
policy I knew only by hearsay; had never been in the society of a
member of Parliament or set foot in either Assembly or Council; had
never heard a political speech or attended a public meeting of any
kind except that already referred to. It is true that I began to follow
the course of events but it was languidly and without real interest.
I had but the vaguest notions of what the policies of the rival parties
were, had never looked at an Act of Parliament except those required
to pass my examinations. Carlyle and Ruskin had considerably shaken

----

[6] Founded 1854. Purchased by the brothers Ebenezer (d. 1860) and David Syme,
1856. During the nineteenth century the 'radical' (or 'liberal') and protectionist
journal of Victoria.

my faith in the doctrine of 'laissez-faire' and rendered me a supporter of State Education, but if catechized at this time I should have on the whole adopted it so far as to declare myself Free Trader, Land Nationalist, or Republican by choice and staunch advocate of popular rights and the popular control of all constitutional machinery.

Having taken chambers in Temple Court [February 1878] and receiving no business whatever, I beguiled my time by devoting myself to the composition of an elaborate work to be entitled *The History and Philosophy of Poetry*, intended to define it and trace its developments, classify it and lay down canons for its criticism in all its departments. The studies in which this involved me certainly in no way increased my legal attainments, though my knowledge of even the elementary essentials of my profession was as vague as my knowledge of practical politics. The few briefs that came to me were formal or nearly so and those that were not suffered accordingly. It was soon plain that I could not expect to earn even a modest living in this way and my small capital saved during my short business career and by teaching soon ran very low.[7] Naturally enough like most young men capable of nothing in particular and fond of reading, I began to turn to the Press. At this time the star of Ruskin was in the ascendant and I began in imitation of *Modern Painters* to criticize the pictures in our National Gallery with the intention of expounding all their significances to an astonished public. Neither *Argus* nor *Age* however took any notice of my proffered contribution. The *Australasian* and *Leader*[8] had already declined one or two poetical effusions of mine. The *Argus* was then sold at three pence and in consequence assumed and maintained an attitude of supercilious contempt for the penny *Age*. Its demeanour towards aspirants who sought its columns was reputed to be equally lofty.

I obtained an introduction to Mr [David] Syme and after a stormy and painful apprenticeship of six months became a regular contributor to the *Age* and *Leader*. For the first time I was compelled to study questions of the day and to inform myself regarding them. Of course they were treated from the standpoint of the paper, and championing its platform soon made it my own. My scruples as to

[7] Deakin's brief career in teaching and business is related in Walter Murdoch's *Alfred Deakin—A Sketch* (Constable, London, 1923), pp. 23-5.

[8] The *Australasian* and the *Leader*: weekly journals connected with the *Argus* and the *Age* respectively.

state interference easily vanished and gradually I became satisfied
that fiscal interference in the interest of the working classes and their
industries was justifiable and necessary. For the time I held my
judgment in suspense, but having the task of replying to the *Argus*
continually thrown upon me, became satisfied of the unsoundness
of their arguments and the superiority of those by which I to my own
satisfaction overthrew them. This was the only article upon which at
first I foresaw a possibility of conflict and was quite prepared to
remain unpledged even if while a journalist I should continue, as
in my [legal] profession, to be the advocate of a cause to which I
was in my own person opposed.

Some years afterwards one of the proprietors of the *Argus* expressed
regret that they had allowed Pearson and myself to slip out of
their hands, quite overlooking the fact that even Pearson, who was
and continued to be a Free Trader, must have written against all his
other convictions upon more important and living issues if he had
joined their staff. In 1879 the Free Trade cause was out of court and
hopeless. The only question was of higher or lower protective duties,
and it was far less uncongenial to consent to increases of ten per cent
or fifteen per cent than to have been ranged against the whole of
the Liberal programme with which in other respects he was strongly
in sympathy. In my own case there was no difficulty at all when I
was once satisfied that state interference if wise was beneficial. Dis-
putes as to the particular levies to be made upon imports were
evidently to be determined according to the merits of each case. The
one remanet of my Free Trade teachings was a conviction that while
Protection was judicious the undue or unnecessary increase of duties
tended towards monopoly and was to be resisted on that score. Of
Prohibition I was from first to last the outspoken antagonist. My
policy was to support the lowest duty which would enable local
industries to sustain a competition with the outside world, imposing
it only upon those classes of products for which our country, climate
and circumstances offered natural advantages and promised a permanent output of sufficient extent to render state action profitable.

The *Age* was at that time and since a doctrinaire paper, its proprietor Mr David Syme having with logical precision and power
deduced his political creed from first principles in the fashion common
to radicals since the days of the French Revolution. Himself without any experience of responsible office or parliamentary life, he

approached his readers from an abstract standpoint by appeals to such doctrines as human equality and the right of the majority to rule, demanding mechanical perfection in the means by which it should assert its supremacy. This was therefore just the field for a young man just as theoretical and with no more experience of practical politics than his chief. When once I had learned to prune to some extent an overflowing style, acquired a knowledge of the facts and arguments relating to matters of local interest, and brought myself continuously in touch with the details in which both the brothers Syme delighted, I became a trusted and indeed favourite contributor and also their personal friend. Still my thoughts were bent upon literature as my ultimate goal and in the vague visions of the future which floated before me there was nothing like a definite political aim.

The *Age* office was then a narrow dirty building in Elizabeth Street[9] where its editorial department shared a single dingy upstairs room, while Mr George Syme edited the *Leader* in the middle of the machine room, separated from it only by a low partition excluding nothing of its constant heat and smells or its frequent working clash and clang. Here bestriding its hearth rug there introduced himself to me Mr W. M. K. Vale, a former newsagent who had risen while yet a youth to the front rank as a stump orator and afterwards to be a member of Parliament and Minister renowned for his democratic proclivities, his strict adherence to total abstinence and its platform, and for his ever bitter tongue. Spirited and ambitious, he had proceeded to England where admission to the Bar was then much easier than in the colonies; and having qualified had just returned to commence professional work and resume in due season his political career. He was a handsome man, well-featured, with fine eyes and a ringing mellow voice, abounding in energy, voluble, fairly well-read and a strict Puritan in life and ideals, strong in domestic affections and susceptible to all their ties. His faults were an egotism which made him envious and suspicious, a biliousness which made him intolerant and vindictive and a vocabulary which made him a master of personal abuse. He had learned much from Higinbotham whom he reverenced more than any human being, though to praise even him or hear him praised was painful to his

9 The *Age* office was moved to Collins Street in 1879.

jealous disposition. He was bright, vivacious, keen, restless and changeable in temper, making few friends and many enemies but commanding respect by his ability, his energy and his ruthless tongue. This chance acquaintance led to a proposition on his part to share the room in Temple Court which I then occupied and thus relieve me of half its cost.[10] The relief to my means scarcely compensated for the burden of his company and conversation, which became monotonous by its restriction to the two themes of his own achievements in word and deed and the demerits of all other public men. But it led to my beginning a political career at a time and in a direction which otherwise I should never have essayed. Probably the work I had commenced would sooner or later have sucked me into the maelstrom of party warfare somewhere else but scarcely in such a striking fashion or with such notable results.

The death of Mr J. T. Smith [30 January 1879] created a vacancy in the constituency known as West Bourke,[11] which stretched from the small metropolitan suburbs of Flemington and Essendon northward through Sunbury and the rich Lancefield district to the dividing range and along its slopes through Macedon and Gisborne to the once famous but then declining gold fields of Blackwood. Thence following the Pentland Hills southward, embracing Bacchus Marsh and Melton, at Keilor it touched the town again. The population of Flemington consisted of artisans and labouring men. Essendon was aristocratic, with many villas. The stretch of country over the Keilor plains and up the Pentland Hills was devoted to grazing. Romsey, Lancefield, part of Gisborne and Bacchus Marsh were richly agricultural and well-cultivated, while the hills of Blackwood were occupied by miners, fossickers and sawmill employees. The great variety of interests embraced, the strength of the Catholic vote in its centre, the large area comprised and its neighbourhood to Melbourne combined to make the district one of the most conspicuous in the colony. The fact that parties appeared to be of about equal strength attracted much interest to it and just at this time the reaction against the Berry Ministry being at its height rendered its capture all-important to the Conservative Opposition,[12] straining

10 Later Vale also shared rooms with Deakin in Selborne Chambers, Chancery Lane.

11 West Bourke returned two members, the other at this time being Donald Cameron, who had been returned at the head of the poll at the election of May 1877, with Smith second in a field of four candidates.

12 Graham Berry had assumed office with a large Liberal majority on 21 May 1877.

every nerve in the endeavour to defeat and discredit the Ministry, whose head had just [28 December 1878] left for London accompanied by Professor Pearson to invoke the intervention of the British Government on behalf of its proposals for Constitutional Reform which had been rejected by the Council, though carried through the Assembly by large majorities.

To win such a seat at such a moment would it was thought discount the embassy to England on its arrival. An exceptionally strong candidate, Mr Robert Harper, a resident in the constituency and a local councillor of one of its shires, was selected to contest it in the Opposition interest and at once commenced an active and vigorous campaign.[13] No Ministerial candidate was forthcoming though a number were named and some issued addresses, but they were either too little known or held opinions which the Liberals could not support. Having vainly searched the district for a man who could be matched against Mr Harper in what was apparently a hopeless struggle, a deputation came at last to Melbourne from the local Reform Leagues in search of a candidate.[14] Among others they invited Mr Vale and waiting for him in my rooms made my acquaintance and obtained my assistance, for what it was worth, in preferring their request. After taking a night to consider and having carefully weighed the prospects of success he declined what was in all eyes becoming a forlorn hope. The Central Reform League was likely to choose its candidate from among its own small coterie whom the deputation were resolved not to accept, believing them all to be incapable of winning so composite and difficult a constituency. They consulted Mr Syme who had probably recommended Vale to them and who having exhausted his list of availables suggested me. Back they came with their utterly unlooked-for request, which after a

[13] Harper's address to the electors was published on 5 February, less than a week after J. T. Smith's death, and vigorously criticized in an *Age* leader of the same date. His first meeting was held at Gisborne that evening.

[14] In her thesis, 'The Economic and Political Development of Victoria, 1877-1881', Ch. XI, Dr J. E. Parnaby discusses the various political Leagues of the time. Leagues to advocate land and constitutional reform, protection or free trade, had been formed since the fifties. They were concerned to persuade voters to enrol and to support candidates professing the appropriate policy. Three were formed in the mid-seventies—the Protection League, mainly representing Melbourne manufacturers; the National Reform League, representing selectors and miners; and the Free Trade League, supported by Melbourne merchants and some pastoralists. Berry achieved amalgamation of the Protection League and the National Reform League during the election of 1877. Dr Parnaby shows that the local branches were particularly jealous of their right to choose their own candidates.

brief interview with Mr Syme who offered to secure Ministerial aid
for election expenses I accepted. The same night [7 February 1879]
the Central Reform League held an angry meeting at which its
disappointed aspirants raged vainly against the *Age* but did not
venture to contest its nomination. My candidature was announced
next morning and next evening I took the platform [at Flemington].
Thus without warning, without ambition, without preparation, without funds or friends, without ever having set foot in the constituency,
without knowing its extent, its centres or even its boundaries, without ever having made a political speech or attended a public meeting, at the age of twenty-two I was suddenly whirled into politics
to wage a desperate and almost hopeless conflict against an adversary
of exceptional ability and claims upon this most difficult seat.

2

'POWER ACTUALLY DESPOTIC'

Graham Berry and his Government, 1877-9

WHATEVER THE RELATIVE IMPORTANCE or interest of the years 1875-82 may be, it is certain that the tide of political life ran then much more fiercely than at any subsequent period. The struggle of 1865 had aroused cries of frantic apprehension from the Conservatives and these were revived with even greater bitterness in the later contest between the same parties. In both instances it must be postulated that the strife was political only—perhaps social too in a modified degree—but little affecting the bulk of the community which went on its way making or trying to make money and amusing itself mainly in spending or sometimes in saving it, little excited by the storm raging at Parliament House or occasional public meetings. Yet placidly busy as business people were, and absorbed as usual in their private loves, hates and rivalries, they were more stirred then than at any time afterwards, attended more meetings, cheered and groaned more lustily and voted in larger percentages.

The real underlying issue was clear. On the one side were the propertied classes, squatters and other capitalists, the land-owners opposed to free selection and desiring to pervert the provisions intended to encourage settlement so as to allow them to accumulate large areas of the public estate, and the merchants who wished that the imports upon which they made their profits should be admitted as far as possible free from duties. These directly interested classes with their bankers constituted the backbone of the Conservative party, behind and around whom were ranged the civil service except its poorest paid members, the professions and the trades people who thrived upon their relationships with the well-to-do. The timid, the prosperous, the pensioners and the remittance men—in fact the dependent members of the community—followed the same lead. Sir James McCulloch, a former leader of the democratic party, himself a wealthy importer, was their chief, having attained that position by overthrowing the Kerferd Ministry though it reigned in

11

[the same] interest, and after it a short-lived Berry Ministry. He was thus enabled to secure the Premiership for himself, taking into his Cabinet most of the members of the Kerferd administration whom he had so recently displaced.[1] He had however to reckon with the ablest of the late Ministers, Mr James Service, whom this transparent piece of political perfidy, executed by McCulloch solely in his own interest, placed in a position of immense advantage before the public, and made him his independent and remorseless critic. With this single exception however, the Conservative party stood solid in 1875-6 behind McCulloch. Its one popular 'plank' was the maintenance of the Education Act[2] though the rest of its programme was in no serious sense reactionary; its Ministry was able and most distinctly respectable but it was little respected and not at all trusted by the masses, who realized that it represented interests opposed to their own, held office as the fruit of a disreputable party intrigue and was kept Liberal only by fear of the consequences of any other policy. In spite of Mr Service's powerful challenge, it went to the general election of [11] May 1877 as confident as Edward II and his noblemen went to meet Bruce at Bannockburn, its mentor the *Argus* prophesying victory, and with no apprehension among its following of the coming overthrow.

The Liberal party consisted of the selectors or farmers who aspired to see their sons selectors, of the manufacturers and artisans who believed that they would be benefited by a Protective tariff, and of the miners who without direct interest—for their families' sake and on patriotic grounds—allied themselves with their working brethren. With these classes it was a matter of measures and not of men, and they went to the poll to vote for the Opposition without criticizing too closely the credentials of those of that party who sought their suffrages. This combination alone was sufficient to turn the scale against any government if, as in this case, people went to the poll; but as in addition the Catholic vote was cast against the Ministry (in accordance with its consistent policy of ousting every Govern-

---

[1] G. B. Kerferd's Ministry assumed office 21 July 1874, retired 7 August 1875; Graham Berry's succeeded, and retired 20 October 1875; McCulloch's succeeded, and retired 21 May 1877.

[2] After long controversy an Act of 1870 (34 Vic. No. 391) abolished state aid to religion as from the end of 1875; and an Act of 1872 (36 Vic. No. 447)—'The Education Act' of this and later references—set up a system of free, compulsory and secular (primary) education. Schools were to be built throughout the colony, and a Department of Education presided over by a Minister of the Crown was created.

ment that would not concede its claims to a grant of public money for its denominational schools) the defeat became annihilation.

Mr Graham Berry assumed office with the largest majority ever seen behind a Victorian Premier. His own career was in many respects analogous to that of Sir Henry Parkes, except that he was a Cockney while Parkes came from an agricultural stock. Berry, like Parkes, had been obliged to leave school at the age of eleven with the three R's, and to commence at once to earn his living. As youngest apprentice in a grocer's shop it was his lot to wait upon the others at lunch and satisfy himself with their leavings. Having torn his only coat, it became the cause of an appeal to his master which resulted in his first increase of salary. He was not an idle apprentice though his taste for reading tempted him often from his task. As a child he had learned to secrete himself with his favourite books in a little closet or cellar under the stair where he could read while the door was ajar, holding it by a string which he drew whenever a footstep warned him of an approach to his cover. His earliest self-denial arose from his setting aside a part of his small wages to buy a coveted copy of Gibbon's *Rome*—not an ordinary taste for a lad behind a counter. *Chambers' Magazine* became to him as to many others his chief source of information, while his taste for poetry which remained with him into manhood was chiefly gratified by Pope. His excellent memory enabled him to retain his favourite passages with little difficulty and when a young man he learned the whole of the *Essay on Man* in fragments while shaving and could still repeat passages from it forty years after. He was somewhat shy and solitary in habit and rejoiced in a three or four mile walk during the whole of which he repeated his favourite verses. In later life Browning's dramas were among his favourite reading. In perseverance, energy, literary taste and poverty of beginnings he resembled Parkes; and like him left the mother country young, passing his thirtieth birthday on board ship. After some experience in his old trade, which corresponded to Parkes' toyshop, he too launched into journalism and though upon a smaller scale about as successfully as Parkes.[3] He was less fortunate

[3] Berry arrived in Melbourne in 1852, and for a while kept a general store in Prahran. He acquired interests in the *Collingwood Observer* and later the *Geelong Register*. Henry Parkes had been apprenticed to a bone and ivory turner, and after his emigration to Sydney in 1839 for some years engaged in this work, selling also toys and fancy goods. He founded and for some years (1850-8) edited the *Empire*, a daily newspaper of considerable merit but not a financial success.

in his endeavours to find a footing in public life and less appreciated
when after several failures he made his first entry. Both had natural
gifts of oratory far beyond the ordinary, disguised under imperfec-
tions of speech and manner. Both scattered their h's wildly and incon-
sistently across their speech, both were egotistic, self-assertive, original
and ambitious.

A strain of cautious conservatism led Berry to oppose the Education
Act as likely to be too costly if the schools were free and as involv-
ing too great a revolution in existing methods. He faced unpopularity,
ridicule and contempt, surviving them all, as well as serious charges
made against his moral character which, like Parkes' financial difficulties, would have wrecked less potent characters. Gradually he
added clearness to his force of style and mastered his vocabulary so
as to become intelligible to all and conquer those passionate out-
bursts which were at the outset mistaken for obscurity of thought
and incapacity of expression. His early career in the Assembly abound-
ed in blunders and there were few to notice that some of them arose
because he was more far-sighted and resourceful than his fellows.
It was palpable that he was needy and aspiring, subordinating his
principles to his eagerness for recognition. It was not observed how
rapidly he was educating himself and how strong a combination he
possessed of the qualities essential to success. His first Ministry, brief
as was its life, left him thereafter conspicuously chastened and
improved. His first Premiership gave him dignity, self-confidence and
self-control. When he became the unquestioned chief of the state in
1877 it was already recognized how much he had contributed to
the success of his party by his great platform campaign in the country,
and how much above his colleagues he stood in constitutional knowledge and in mastery of the principles of Parliamentary government.
Self-indulgent, vain, governed largely by personal attachments, and
without other ideals than those of his class, he was at the same time
genuine in the fervour of his devotion to the cause of the people and
had become both by energy and ability remarkable even among
the most distinguished colonial politicians. He gradually grew
polished and polite, of a settled gravity which did not exclude a
sense of humour, with a deep sense of the importance of his position
and a resolute determination to make his tenure of it memorable and
if possible permanent. He developed his powers by their practice;
all his knowledge was real and gained from life instead of from

books; he was alive to his finger tips, quickly sympathetic with a crowd or with the House, a master of tactics, cool headed in the height of his fury and with instinctive insight into the weak points of an opponent's case or the salient advantages of his own. It was a public misfortune that Mr Service did not join him in 1877 and bring to the task before the Ministry his sober, cautious and consistent judgment of men and things, and the possibilities of the hour.

Berry's colleagues though vigorous and strong were all more radical, more factious and less public-spirited than himself. Grant was one of the best educated, best mannered and sagest, though weak, and he was accustomed to say that his proper period was the French Revolution when he could have seen the heads of the aristocrats rolling upon the scaffold. Sir Bryan O'Loghlen who became his Attorney-General was an Irish barrister, most amiable and upright, but regarding his opponents as Saxon oppressors due to suffer for their past sins against his country.[4] He was sincere and at this time loyal to his principles. His party was in power and must use its opportunities so as to erase its adversaries. Lalor was still the same dashing determined and masterful autocrat, as heedless, desperate and revolutionary as when he headed the Eureka declaration of independence a quarter of a century before. Patterson, full of cunning adaptability and energy, had been a Free Trader with Conservative leanings but, having decided that the people were upon the other side, was prepared to prove his loyalty to his new flag by any action or speech that might seem necessary. Woods, more thoughtful and more consistent, was a Chartist by training to whom restraints of any kind were obnoxious. His opinions were heterodox upon all issues and he had old scores against the wealthy and influential which he was eager to pay off. Longmore, an excellent husband, father and friend, was as bitter, tenacious and intemperate a temperance man as Vale, whom he resembled in his taste for vituperation. He was appropriately enough Minister of Lands, because inspired with all a selector's distrust and all an Irishman's hate of great landlords. W. Collard Smith, one of the more genial and least aggressive of the band, was a shrewd man of the world, dextrous, pliable and kindly, his pleasant address, personal popularity and temporizing disposition being especially useful among such associates. His principles were those which he had found necessary to secure his

---

[4] This sentence has been slightly re-arranged.

seat in Ballarat and his place in the Cabinet, and he had none to
sacrifice in order to adopt them. He was more devoted to his chief
and a better interpreter of the average voter than his fellows. Though
as supple as Longmore was stiff, and as mild as he was harsh,[5] both
were little above the average of the ordinary member or man in the
street. The others were all superior men and abler as individuals than
those whom they had supplanted. They had courage, initiative,
ideas and energy in an uncommon degree, but were deficient in
judgment, tact, delicacy of feeling and sober industry. They were in
their way innovators, experimenters and adventurers, jealous of each
other and co-operating only under pressure of necessity and Berry's
ascendancy, against which Patterson began to plot as soon as he
was able to establish his own position. They were but crude legisla-
tors or administrators from want of the necessary application and
harmony, but excellent fighting men and eager to smite and spare
not.

Their first enterprise was the passage of a Land Tax aimed
at the great estates but unjust in its incidence, which the Council
did not dare to veto, revenging itself however by rejecting the Payment of Members Bill. The Ministry had already independently
included in the Appropriation Bill the sum necessary to give effect
to the measure when the Council in its turn, fully conscious of the
seriousness of the step it was taking, rejected the measure. After a
long interval Victoria was plunged into another deadlock. The
public servants remained unpaid, the Conservatives rejoicing at the
burden imposed upon the Ministry, and the Council comfortably
prepared to starve them out. They provoked the contest without
apprehensions for themselves, chortling at the deprivation of salary
to which they were subjecting their opponents. They had been compelled to consent to a Land Tax which hit and hit hard practically
every member of their body and they now determined to hit back
as hard and as long as they could at those representatives of the
electors who had dared to touch their pockets. They had not calcu-
lated with Mr Berry or his Cabinet and their awakening to the fact
that they had to deal with men who could not be trifled with was
abrupt, utterly unexpected, and provocative of feelings of dismay

----

[5] The original has 'stiff as Longmore was supple, and harsh as he was mild', but
the context shows clearly that the order of the adjectives should have been that given
above.

Sir Graham Berry

and terror, of stupefaction and rage which made the beginning of 1878 forever memorable in Victorian history.

What the Government did was to announce that in consequence of the stoppage of supplies by the Council it was impossible for them to maintain a public service which was overmanned and in its higher ranks overpaid. Consequently without a word of warning a list of County Court Judges, Police Magistrates and other civil servants were dismissed.[6] The choice of the persons discharged in the departments was left to individual Ministers and but roughly revised by the Cabinet. A few of those who were given *congé* were selected on the advice of their superiors because they were below the standard of competency or industry of their fellows, and a larger number because they occupied what were practically sinecures, but there were some who were picked because they were in receipt of high salaries and suspected of being in sympathy with the Conservatives. They were in the way of the new Ministers and, though highly capable officers, were dismissed in a few cases, it is to be feared, from private motives and not for public ends. The general effect of the blow was instantaneous. The whole service, hitherto somewhat supercilious in its attitude to a radical administration, was at once brought to its knees in abject submission. The Opposition shrieked but trembled and began to talk of compromise. The electors as a whole remained unmoved, ardent partisans applauding or condemning according to their party ties, but on the whole a tacit approval was given to the reprisals. The Council began to prepare to surrender and the Ministry paused.

The ultras who had tasted blood were eager for more. Lalor, the ringleader, foresaw another and more successful Eureka rising in which he would control the public services. His programme was to close the Custom House and thus by stopping all imports introduce a policy of Prohibition which would threaten the merchants with ruin. He was further prepared if necessary to stop the Post Office and the Railways so as to paralyse the whole business of the country, to forbid the issue of notes by the banks and to replace them by a state paper currency. He hinted darkly also at a possible dismissal of the warders and throwing open of gaols and asylums for the

[6] The announcement of the dismissals was made in a supplement to the *Government Gazette* issued on the evening of 8 January 1878. The next day was known as 'Black Wednesday', a phrase recalling the catastrophe of 'Black Thursday' (6 February 1851) when bushfires devastated the colony.

C

insane should the Council persist in its recalcitrance. He was quite
ready to govern the colony with the assent of the Assembly alone.
The plates for the new notes were, it is said, already in course of
preparation.[7] The minor courts were to be closed and others would
follow. What was projected was in point of fact a Revolution which
was not to close until the Council was reformed out of existence by a

---

[7] It will be noticed that this sketch of a revolutionary plot cannot rest upon direct
contemporary knowledge. In January 1878 Deakin had no personal acquaintance with
Members of Parliament. He would undoubtedly in later years have heard much about
the crisis from some of those who had been concerned in it, but nevertheless the
passage does not constitute first-hand evidence. He himself would at the time have
heard the rumours of extreme actions to come, for there was plenty of talk about them.
But ominous talk at such a time is to be expected; whether such positive actions as
the actual preparation of a greenback issue were taken is more doubtful. Lalor and
some other Berryites had certainly used something like 'revolutionary' language in
public speeches, and some of their references to the banks would have been sufficient,
in the atmosphere of the time, to start rumours about a proposed issue of 'greenbacks'
which could have seemed plausible. Thus a letter to the *Argus* (11 January 1878)
said that a Minister of the Crown [probably Lalor] had stated it to be his intention
to 'shut up the —— banks by making them pay in gold'. Lalor at this time was threatening to coerce the mercantile interests who were alleged to be behind the Legislative
Council by stopping the carriage of goods on the Hobson's Bay railway, stopping the
payment of drawbacks to merchants and stopping the payment of mining royalties.
'If we make things short, sharp and decisive enough, they [the Council] will see the
wisdom of repenting of their evil ways before a dissolution need take place' (*Argus*,
19 January 1878). A. T. Clark, a Berry supporter in the Assembly, and later a Minister,
said about the same time, 'In the coming struggle let the banks be the victims, for
virtually they are the Council. . . . Next Monday we hope to hear that money, so called,
in the shape of banknotes will not be recognized. Gold alone will be received, and
that must be paid into the national Treasury' (quoted from the *Williamstown
Advertiser* in the *Argus*, 'Summary for Europe', 23 January 1878). Statements such
as this may have been responsible for the rumours about 'greenbacks', which however
do not seem to have been taken seriously for very long. There is no real hostility in the
interjection by Service in the course of a statement in Parliament by Berry about the
advancing of credit to selectors: 'Issue a lot of greenbacks and the thing can be done
at once (Laughter)' (*Argus*, 7 March 1878). But after the first shock of the Civil
Service dismissals rumour had certainly been busy, as the frantic leaders of the *Argus*
show. The Governor felt it necessary to write a Memorandum for Ministers stating
that he 'would strongly recommend Ministers (as he has already recommended the
Premier) to take measures for publicly contradicting the false rumours that have been
circulated to the effect that the Government contemplates some interference with the
currency and the banking institutions. . . . Moreover (as was communicated to the
Premier some time back) the Governor is precluded by the Queen's instructions from
sanctioning any measure of that nature . . . the Governor is prohibited from giving
his assent to measures whereby any paper or other currency may be made a legal
tender, except the coin of the realm, or other gold or silver coin' (Memorandum of
22 January 1878, quoted in S. Lane-Poole (ed.), *Thirty Years of Colonial Government*
(London, 1889), II. 96-7). Further evidence is needed before it can be believed that
the plates for the new notes were actually in the course of preparation. In later years
the rumour could have gained plausibility by recollection of the apparently convincing
'Fascimile of the Government Greenbacks that were being prepared for issue in January
1878' included as an illustration (p. 19) in the hostile satire published by Melbourne
Punch, 'The History of the Berry Ministry' [1879]. Dr. Parnaby's thesis, 'The Economic
and Political Development of Victoria, 1877-1881', has nothing to add on these points.

reign of terror. Lalor, Patterson, Woods, and Longmore were the active participants in this wild plot, to which O'Loghlen might have succumbed and by which even Grant was for the moment tempted, had it not been for the resolute refusal of Mr Berry (probably affected to some extent by the appeals of the alarmed Governor) to take a single step more than was necessary to secure his end. The party was evidently at his back. Mass meetings began to be held in the metropolis at which menacing language was employed. I remember seeing a vacant space in Collins Street, I think where Glen's Music Shop now [1900] stands, crowded with a great body of men cheering speakers who addressed them in support of the Ministry from platforms improvised on vans and lit by flaring grease lamps and torches. On the opposite side of the street where the Athenaeum Club stood, Mr J. L. Purves, then member for Mornington, was endeavouring to address a part of the mob who hurled not only their groans and cries but stones at him until he was dragged inside and out of danger by his friends.[8] The temper of the people was evidently becoming kindled by the exciting incidents, uncertainties and rumours of the hour; and on the whole it was clear that both town and country were against the Council. As a consequence it ignominiously surrendered.

It is unnecessary to enter into the question how far the Governor, Sir George Bowen, did or did not exceed his functions in consenting to the wholesale dismissals though his demeanour during the crisis was certainly unfortunate. What he did and said, and what was said of him, are matters of history.[9] What is not generally known is that he not only cordially supported his Cabinet but at the time was prepared to endorse the severest measures proposed by the most extreme members of the Cabinet. He was ready to close the Railways one day, the Post Office the next and the Gaols on the third, and openly said so. Afterwards he became alarmed at his own indiscretions and quailed before the storm which he had helped to raise, becoming as much a source of embarrassment to his Ministers by his terrors as he had been in his reckless hours. A strong and wise man in his position would have consented only to temporary suspensions of the public servants, and have insisted upon guarantees

[8] The *Argus*, 1 February 1878, gives an account of this incident.
[9] Bowen's despatches, and other documents dealing with the crisis in Victoria, are printed in *British Parliamentary Papers*, 1878, LVI; 1878-9, LI; and in S. Lane-Poole (ed.), *Thirty Years of Colonial Government* (London, 1889), vol. II, ch. XXIV-XXVII.

that the public should not be made to suffer more than was absolutely
necessary by any interference with the services upon which they
depended. It was not Sir George Bowen's fault that there was not
a revolution. Berry admitted in his later years that 'Black Wednesday' had been a mistake because it had mixed retrenchment in the
public service with a blow at the Council. It was fortunate that he
did not advise still more drastic measures than those actually adopted,
for had he done so they would certainly have been counter-signed by
the Governor who at the time imposed no check whatever upon his
Ministers. Berry was not habitually violent even in speech in regard
to individuals, institutions or even parties. The one occasion on which
he became centre of a scene was when as a leader of the Opposition
he referred to Sir Charles MacMahon as a 'Corrupt Speaker'. As a
matter of fact he had no intention of doing so; but losing the thread
of his speech owing to the interruptions to which he was subject,
and having just before read a newspaper article in which the phrase
was used, he drifted into its repetition before he was well aware of
it and afterwards would not withdraw it. He was really the most
conservative man in his own Ministry of 1877-80.

   The first after-consequence of the struggle with the Council was
the introduction of a Bill to reform the Upper House by limiting its
authority over financial measures and providing that all other Bills,
after being twice rejected, might be referred to a direct vote of the
people (then generally termed a plebiscite). This measure was passed
in the Assembly [8 October 1878] only to be rejected in the Council,
whereupon Mr Berry accompanied by Professor Pearson set out for
London to submit the position to the Secretary of State for the
Colonies, Sir Michael Hicks-Beach, and enquire what support might
be expected from the British Government if the Council still continued obdurate and deliberately refused to bow to the will of the
majority. This mission was afterwards admitted by Berry to have
been 'a wild goose chase' into which he would never have been drawn
but for Bowen's duplicity. For reasons of his own the Governor,
according to Berry, concealed from the Ministry his receipt of despatches in regard to the embassy which if they had been seen by
him would have prevented its ever setting out. He used to say too
that when in London he was met by the hostility of the banks seeking for partly political reasons to render his proposed loan a failure,
and that he had to take the sole responsibility of raising its minimum

two per cent. Sir A. Michie, then Agent-General for the colony, ignored his presence in London and he was obliged to enter his office and capture so to speak the Chair of the Board of Advice to deal with the tenders. The success of the loan was his own.

It was while they were absent that the vacancy in West Bourke occurred for which I became a candidate under the conditions here portrayed in brief. The feeling of the electors was still aroused. The Opposition, smarting under their reverses and stimulated by the victims from the civil service (none of whom had been restored to office though the Appropriation Bill had since been passed), were nevertheless still depressed. The Ministerialists were triumphant and aggressive. When Berry returned with the intimation—which certainly needed no Embassy for its acquisition—that we must exhaust all means of settling our own differences before seeking Imperial intervention, he was received with as much enthusiasm as if he had descended from a Sinai with tables of stone containing new commandments. On the night of his return [17 June 1879] Collins Street was packed from Spencer Street Station to the old Treasury and he was driven from one to the other in a carriage, surrounded by a torchlight procession and accompanied by rolling volleys of cheers. He addressed the crowd from a balcony in the Chief Secretary's Office next to that on which I was stationed; and it was here that I first saw this celebrated leader, flushed with excitement but completely self-controlled, declaring with a voice hoarse partly with the strain of endeavouring to reach the packed thousands before him and partly with the passion of his popular harangues, that he had brought them 'Peace with Honour'. The crowd, evidently entirely satisfied to trust him, thundered its applause. It was a great homecoming, a real demonstration, the greatest probably he had ever received or ever was to receive, and it marked the zenith of his career. His power was at that moment and for some time before and after actually despotic. His colleagues were all classed in public opinion far below him. He was the central figure both in the House and in the country and knew it well.

He was above the middle height and well-proportioned except that his shoulders sloped a little and his legs were slightly bent outwards. He was of strong frame, well-fleshed but not corpulent and of pleasant smile. His head was high, without angles, rather large and rounded; his grey eyes were full, prominent and expressive;

the nose a little too thick; the forehead high and well-shaped; the chin straight; the cheek bones rather high; with great variability of countenance when excited. His hands were large and spatulous and gesticulating even in conversation when he became moved, though he was self-controlled and capable of remaining in repose. Everything about him was alive and eloquent and full of purpose when he was really roused. He afforded an excellent contrast to Higinbotham when I saw them sitting on each side of the President of the Trades Hall at the opening of its new Council Chamber in 1884. The Chief Justice's profile was cameo-like in its delicacy, refinement and finish; his full face judicial, broad-browed and square-jawed; his blue eyes clear, still, calm and far-seeing when not ablaze with passion. There was a mildness and sweetness in his manner, tone and carriage which were cherubic. Their styles of speech were as contrasted: Higinbotham's slower, grander, more stately and impressive, with far more dignity in style and grace of phrase, yet terribly intense and effective in its admirable climaxes. Berry was swifter, ruder, plainer, clumsier but far more practical and of every-day consideration; less lofty, less ideal but much nearer to the average man's business and bosom. To see and hear them was to understand them and their careers—the great Liberal Orator and the great Liberal Leader, one completing the other.

When I was introduced to him a day or so after [his return from England] Berry was suffering from gout in his right hand and could only offer his left. His English experiences had impressed him though not so as to render him more popular. He was to all calm, superior, almost distant in his demeanour as became the dictator of Victoria. He afterwards said to me, 'Yes, I then had absolute power, but only upon the one condition that I did not use it.' Spirited, vigorous, resourceful, self-confident, the leader of a great majority in the Assembly and in the electorates, he was without question at that time endowed with capacity and authority such as rarely falls to any man in a self-governing community and which can only exist in such a community. Every eye was fixed upon him, every paper devoted its columns to discussing him, every public gathering debated and almost every private meeting argued about him. Carica-tured, traduced and slandered by the Conservatives, he was almost idolized by the masses and obediently followed by his supporters, even by those who like some of his Cabinet were only too willing to push him from his place if they could see a chance of succeeding him but who realized that he was still indispensable and irremovable. He embodied the sentiments of a considerable section of the people which looked to him to do its work of reform and reorganization, while he led a great number of others captivated either by his speeches or his acts or worshippers of the risen sun. The intensity of the hate cherished for him by the opposing faction was almost inexpressible, and his assassination seemed at this time a not-too-impossible contingency in view of the threats showered upon him by those whom he had taxed, out-manoeuvred, dismissed or defeated. His true safety lay in the fact that he had the bulk of the people actually behind him and around him; the best of bodyguards if not the most permanent.

'GAY IRRESPONSIBILITY'

The Election for West Bourke, 1879

THE GAY IRRESPONSIBILITY with which I entered upon the contest for West Bourke was obviously very different from the gravity with which my opponent pursued his long-prepared design. A man about ten years my senior, he had with the assistance of his brothers built up a considerable business in coffee, spices and the like, and was well-known to many farmers of the district as a purchaser of their chicory. The firm had a reputation for smartness, and their opponents said for sharp practices, but all its members were young, capable and energetic. With means, some leisure and good natural capacity, Robert Harper had been able to complete what was considered a good education, to marry a daughter of the chief Presbyterian clergyman of Melbourne [Dr Cairns] and to occupy a distinguished place in the powerful Presbyterian body and in society. His country house was at Macedon and residence there had enabled him to enter into the Shire Council as a stepping stone for Parliament. He had some experience in municipal affairs and practice in public speaking, many friends and hosts of acquaintances throughout the district which he knew well except in its mining portions. A man of keen intelligence, well-informed on political questions, of strong character, great persistency, marked resoluteness and untiring energy, he not unreasonably considered that he merited the seat not only by his local knowledge and services, but as superior to all his rivals in the field.

He was lacking only in one quality to which I had some claim and this was a sense of humour. When it happened during our second contest that we came to spend a night in the same hotel at Romsey and breakfasted together, he occupied most of the time with a careful contrast of our relative positions, capacities and prospects. While he admitted that I might be a clever journalist and promising but briefless barrister with some aptitude for the platform, he was convinced that it must be clear to me how much these qualifications of mine were outweighed by his fuller and longer experience in business and in municipal matters, his financial independence and social standing. I was still a juvenile theorist with unformed character and immature opinions, needing only an interval of steady application to acquire riper knowledge and thus gradually become fit to aspire to a seat in the legislature. He on the other hand was ready and qualified now, with an established position and reputation, accustomed to deal with men and things, and prepared to bear the burden of responsibility as a representative. I had everything to learn and it would be much better for me if I completed my education in a private station and at leisure instead of under pressure and as a public man, as I must if I succeeded in my candidature. Delicately but firmly he put it to me that in review of the facts I ought to recognize his right to precedence and retire in his favour. The best man ought to win and it ought not to be left to the chances of an election to pick the winner. He was the best man. My duty was plain. On the last point I was compelled to disagree with him because of party obligations. We were not the only two persons to be considered in the matter. Of course he did not ask me to resign but this was the inevitable conclusion of his argument. He left it to me dispassionately. The humour did not lie in any travesty of the facts on his part. The comparison between us was perfectly just and certainly did not underestimate my claims. He was superior in all the particulars he mentioned and I should have been the better for the period of incubation which he recommended. The fun lay in the circumstance that it was he who expounded this to me while we were rival candidates for the seat.

My equipment was certainly very insufficient. I had read largely upon abstract politics and had written a good deal upon their local application but all this was mere journalistic disquisition. Necessarily I had not had time or opportunity to test the formulas which I accepted or to study their adaptation to local circumstances. I knew nothing at first hand about either colony or constituency, had hardly ever been out of Melbourne, and was profoundly ignorant of the great industries and sources of production upon which our prosperity depended. Of the conditions of the sister colonies, our rivals and co-operators, or of the world relations which we were together building up and with whose requirements we were bound to comply, I knew

nothing clearly. I probably possessed a great deal more acquaintance
with first principles than most candidates but certainly knew a great
deal less about practical life and affairs. I was still an overgrown lad
looking at least five years older than I was, whose sporting instincts
were roused by the excitement of a contest and whose love of
adventure led him to regard the whole campaign as something of a
picnic combined with a platform competition with my adversary
and my audiences which at first amused me for its own sake. Of the
machinery of an election I knew absolutely nothing, never having
voted or entered a polling booth or belonged to a committee or canvassed or taken any part in such contests. Naturally I was in the
hands of friends and allies. My very address was not my own, being
written down by me at the offhand dictation of the Editor of the
Age, Mr Windsor, who at once assumed the direction of that func-
tion. Needless to say I welcomed his aid, both to propitiate him and
because his style was so much more nervous and vigorous than
my own. Its substance was mine as it was his because at that time
it expressed the policy of the paper in which we were both expounding it daily. It appeared on the Saturday morning [*Age*, 8 February
1879] and on the same evening I was to make my first appearance
on a political platform and my first bow to the electors of West
Bourke. I threw together the materials for my speech in the morning
and rested in the afternoon, having somehow acquainted myself
with the position of the place at which I was to speak. It was a small
shire hall not seating more than 100 people and providing standing
room for as many more, or perhaps 250 in all.[1] It was packed to the
doors although the notice was so short and this part of the district
was then sparsely settled, the crowd being drawn partly I think
because of the curiosity aroused by the first appearance of an utterly
unknown young man who was described in the *Argus* as a leading-
article writer for the *Age*.

Although relying almost wholly upon my memory for these
sketches I have looked up the *Age* report of the speech then delivered.[2]
At first beginning in an agony of nervousness, as indeed is my
general experience up to the present time, but soon attaining sufficient
command of myself to follow out the line of exposition determined
upon, I flung myself (so to speak) at my hearers with much enthus-

[1] The Town Hall at Flemington.
[2] *Age*, 10 February 1879.

iasm. My voice was described as pleasant, the enunciation very clear but extremely rapid, rising according to the reporters to over 200 words a minute for the greater part of my speech, and sometimes to 220-240 and even 250 words a minute when under excitement. There was a good deal of excitement in me then, and in all audiences. At all events the reception of this, my first harangue, with its quotations from Castelar and Macaulay was most inspiriting.[3] Ardent Liberals cheered at every pause; while in replies to interjections and answers to questions I scored, according to their thinking, off my adversaries. Practically, there were four planks in my platform: Reform of the Council, Protection, the Maintenance of the Education Act against the Catholic claims, and defence of the Land Tax. My familiarity with detail obtained in the process of writing about these enabled me to expound my views upon these topics with great readiness and fullness. The majority of those who attend public meetings are rarely seekers after novelties in the shape of ideas. They are well-content to listen to an exposition of current issues and are unduly impressed by fluency of speech and the citation of facts and figures apparently apposite to the text.

The meeting was a great success and its importance much enhanced by the presence on the platform of the Minister of Public Works, Mr Patterson, with whom I then made acquaintance for the first time. He was at this period assiduous in paying court to the *Age* and it was out of deference to the paper and because of my association with it that he attended to give me the Ministerial endorsement. The manner in which he did it was characteristic. Coming out full of zeal, attended by an old friend and political henchman, Mr Gray —a man of simple kindly straightforward disposition with whom I was afterwards more closely connected—his ardour gradually cooled as he reflected upon the possibilities of my proving a failure and the ridicule to which he might be exposed if he attended the meeting of a man whom he knew to be a perfect novice in politics, and who might for all he knew never be able to express himself articulately.

---

3 'The greatest of modern Spanish orators, perhaps the greatest orator of modern times, had said, "Before you ask a reform through the laws, it is necessary to formulate it with clearness, to diffuse it with perseverance, to propagate it by electoral meetings, to take care that from these electoral meetings it shall come up as a mysterious sap into Parliaments, and from Parliaments into Governments".' . . . 'Lord Macaulay had said that there was only one cure for the evils that arose from newly acquired freedom, and that one cure was freedom.'

ALFRED DEAKIN;

Is the only LIBERAL and Ministerial Candidate in West Bourke. He is in favor of

The Ministerial Scheme of Constitutional Reform

Which does away with Deadlocks, obtains finality of Legislation, and places the

Supreme Power in the Hands of the People.

He is in favor of an

Equitable Land Tax,

Of the existing

Education Act,

But with increased Powers to Boards of Advice; of

Protection to Native Industry,

To benefit the farmers by keeping a Market for them free from foreigners. In favor of the NEW LOAN, which will give a great impetus to all trade and business in the Colony; In favor of the

Great Railway Scheme

Of the present Govermnent, which will connect all the districts with the interior of the Seaboard; and in favor of the

Exhibition Bill

Which will display to Strangers the vast resources of Victoria.

Vote for the People's Candidate
Vote for the Liberal Candidate
Vote for the Ministerial Candidate.

Do you want popular Legislation instead of Class legislation? Do you want Money brought into the Colony, Prosperity for the People, and Railways made to your Markets? Do you want Employment and Education for your children?

THEN VOTE FOR

ALFRED DEAKIN.

Printed at the " Chronicle Office." Romsey.

ELECTORS
OF
WEST BOURKE !

The Contest to be fought out to-day at the Ballot Box does not lie between Mr. Harper and Mr. Deakin, but between Conservatism and Liberalism ; the former represents the Merchants, the Importers and the Squatters. The latter represents the Farmers, the Artisans and working men generally, (the bone and sinew, and the intelligence of the land.

Then like brave and true men

Rally Round the Standard

of your own independence, and prevent the power so hardly won from been wrested from your hands, by deep designing men :--Do not be cajoled,

VOTE FOR

Mr. Deakin,

VOTE FOR

Your Homes, Your Families, and Your Adopted Country !!

Printed at the " Chronicle Office," Romsey,

Election Handbills, 1879

Consequently he made for the nearest hotel himself and despatched
Gray to reconnoitre the hall and to return with a report of the size
and character of the gathering and the manner in which I was being
received. Gray was back again in a few moments with the news
(as given me in his own words): 'He's all right. They're cheering
him like mad.' Accordingly Patterson entered, took his seat upon the
platform, and at the conclusion of my remarks addressed the meeting
in the slow, carefully prepared and sledge-hammer style characteristic of him. His matter was not very good and certainly not fresh
but his manner was emphatic, his style forcible and his warmth
infectious. His rather low-jutting forehead, stiff rebellious hair,
strong cheek and jaw bones, twinkling and rather small dark eyes
and powerful frame, rather stooping shoulders and heavy-footed
pace all marked the weight and will of the man. They also pointed
backward to his career as slaughterman and butcher. Beginning by
being barely able to read and write, earning a spare living by hard
physical labour, without any power of speech or knowledge of the
world, he had painfully and laboriously educated himself; making
his first appearance in public at penny readings until slowly and
pertinaciously he made his way into notice but continued ever open
to hints, ever learning and ever improving by imitation, by conversation and by enquiry until he was councillor, member, minister;
and at this time becoming by sheer force of character and brain
one of the leading members of the Government. Sly, tricky and
untrustworthy it is true, but with a fine air of frankness; genial
in personal relations; a good deal of genuine warmth of heart for
his friends; great perceptive powers and a dauntless resolve to rise; his
was no ordinary political aim. The most amusing and characteristic
comment he made that evening was in private and to myself as we
walked away. 'D—— me,' said he, 'if I ever understood this blessed
Plebiscite until you explained it tonight.' This from one of the
authors of the Bill which proposed its adoption as a part of our
Constitution! He was far from blind to the humour of this con-
fession—but one of his strong points was that when it was safe to do
so he liked telling the truth. He was strong enough for that. His
consistent policy was to avail himself of every acquaintance so as to
add to his own store of knowledge. At this time he did not read at
all and at no time did he read more than a very few books. He was
dependent largely upon journalists like the Editor of the *Age*, and

afterwards Mr Willoughby of the *Argus*, for much of the matter and form of his speeches. An assiduous sucker of brains, he was able to employ the materials thus furnished to good advantage, making them his own and setting his mark upon them. His borrowings were continuous but legitimate and well-applied.

On the Monday [10 February 1879] at midday I set off on my campaign, though not having taken the precaution to look at a map my course remained a mystery to me. Leaving the railway at Keilor Road I took the coach through Melton, where two or three Liberals discussed prospects with me while we changed horses, and thence on to Bacchus Marsh where we arrived at evening. I remember the Ruskin and Wordsworth influences inducing me to prepare a word picture of the sunset as I saw it when descending into the valley where the township lay; but which I did not afterwards venture to deliver to the audience of stolid farmers whom I addressed, from a sense of its unsuitability, though I had prided myself in anticipation upon the effect which such an original passage of Turneresque landscape would have created in an electioneering speech. My remarks were well-received and as I had taken care not to repeat much of what had been reported in the *Age* and answered many questions without hesitation and abundant self-confidence the meeting was equally successful.[4] After this and everywhere I found that I was expected to entertain and be entertained at a friendly public house with my leading supporters and to discuss operations with them. As I was a vegetarian, a total abstainer and a non-smoker, I was not the most convivial of beings. Then again, though at this time I was a good sleeper, I was accustomed to retire early; while in the country even more than the town it was thought justifiable to prove good fellowship by drinking and discussing far into the night.[5] Great must have been the disappointment of the many when on the plea of fatigue I retired early, though the Temperance party commenced to rally to me when my habits and practices were better known. Happily, when questioned, I announced myself opposed to Sunday trading in hotels, though I had never really considered the questions involved. At the same time I at once separated myself from

---

4 Reported in *Age*, 11 February 1879.

5 Deakin was no doctrinaire on questions of diet, but he suffered from poor digestion, and tried dietary experiments in seeking relief. He remained a non-smoker, but gave up vegetarianism and total abstinence, though he was always a very moderate drinker. In later years he became a very poor sleeper.

the Ministry in regard to the public servants dismissed during the crisis of 1878, declaring that all ought to have been restored to their positions when the Appropriation Bill was passed by the Council; and that the reductions in the service said to be necessary should then have been made impartially and after careful enquiry into qualifications so as to retain the best and part with the least efficient. In the same way I declined to endorse the existing Land Tax because of its unscientific character and thus began to assert an individuality of view which increased the more I reflected and the better I became aware of the facts. The constant discussion of public affairs of itself began to affect my mind, and so far as I could judge the addresses I delivered were improved as the contest proceeded. It was in itself an event to me to travel alone, to sleep in strange inns without friends or relations near, and much more to see for the first time rural life and manners, its hospitalities and kindnesses.

Next morning I was driven up the beautiful Pentland Hills and revelled in the scenery unfolded before me, while much amused at the bucolic deliberation of those whom I encountered at our stopping places. It was a novelty to me to watch the slow assemblage of a dozen or twenty rough men who rode or drove up and were gradually shepherded into a room provided with a sleepy-looking slow-speaking chairman who introduced me, invited questions, put the vote, and then ordered in refreshments for all on his or my account. I spoke thus at Myrniong, Greendale, then driving over the mountains to Black-wood spoke there at Redhill, finishing by a drive through the darkness to a great meeting of miners at Barry's Reef, reached soon after 9 p.m., where I received a great ovation. Next day, Wednesday [12 February 1879], I was driven through endless woods to Kyneton and took the train to Gisborne, speaking there that evening and driving late at night to Riddell's Creek where I spoke on Thursday midday [13 February 1879] and at Romsey at night; launching myself after each meeting into space, going where I was told, finding someone who could show me the Hall and bring me to the active Liberals of the place, and so from strangers to strangers in an utterly unknown country, wandering in a perpetual whirl of mysterious and novel procedure. At Lancefield Road I was taken in hand by a great, fat, red-faced old warrior named Johnson whose father had fought against the Repeal of the Corn Laws and who was full of interesting stories of the old Loyal Liberal party and its eventful history. At

The Berry-Blight on the Ballot-Box

Sir B. O'L. 'Hollo! Mr Kelly, I'm doing a bit in your line.'

Ned Kelly. 'No, Mr Baronet, *not* in my line. Bad as I am I don't do a widow out of her money, or rob any man of his political rights. I've not taken to that yet.'

Romsey I was taken out of his hands by Kelly, a bank manager of an original type, who was Liberal in politics chiefly because the rival banker was a staunch Conservative; and by a jovial, hearty, kindly, ne'er-do-well auctioneer named Stokes who was extremely popular by reason of his wife's good qualities and his own cheery optimism and sunny good temper.

It was at the close of the Romsey meeting, which concluded auspiciously with the usual vote in my favour, that I was unexpectedly informed that Mr Woods, the Minister of Railways, had arrived with sundry officials to take a preliminary glance at the route of the railway to Lancefield for which the district had long been pleading. Of course the purpose of this sudden appearance of his was to influence votes in my favour; but as it had been devised and carried out entirely without my knowledge, though I felt some compunctions, it was with a certain degree of elation that I went across to my hotel where he had taken up his quarters after looking in at my meeting and satisfying himself of its progress. I found him in a large room filled with a cloud of tobacco smoke and the aroma of whisky and water, his rotund form, snub nose, glistening eyes and spiky hair rendering him a rather Socrates-Silenus in appearance. He hailed me cheerfully as if an old acquaintance though I had never spoken to him or seen him before, and continued his graphic and sometimes epigrammatic comments upon the questions of the day. An originally-minded man, who read a good deal of serious literature, and possessed a rugged character in which the good points about balanced the bad, it was his lack of industry and self-control alone that allowed Patterson to leave him and others like him behind in the race. Egotistical, vain and dogmatic, he had a gift of phrase-making which Patterson envied and by care came to surpass, though nothing he ever coined equalled the vigour of Woods at his best or worst; as when he attacked the Sabbatarians for permitting Sunday trains merely in order that they might take 'the greasy saints to their superstition shops'. He was not sufficiently careful an administrator, though active and thoughtful and taking pride in his work, lacking ballast, tact and judgment in his dealings with officers and members. In consequence he drifted out of touch with his party and was omitted from its subsequent Ministries. At this time he was prominent but, as in this very expedition, reckless and inconsiderate

D

even in his cunning. I did not see him again and had little speech with him.

Friday evening [14 February 1879] found me at Lancefield after making many calls upon leading farmers who insisted upon my eating and drinking in all their houses; and next morning before daylight I was on my way back to Melbourne, leaving the train at Keilor and returning through Tullamarine and Bulla without speaking, to Sunbury, where I concluded a week in which I had addressed ten meetings and travelled on my canvassing more than a couple of hundred miles. On Sunday evening [16 February 1879] I met Sir Bryan O'Loghlen at the *Age* office where he had called to learn what the prospects were of my success. On the Monday evening [17 February 1879] I spoke at Essendon and at Kensington. Tuesday the 18th February [1879] was polling day. My whole campaign had been compressed into eight days although enough had happened in them to make them seem eighty, so great seemed the interval between the first speech and the last, and so crowded were my novel experiences between. At the preceding election Cameron had been returned at the head of the poll with 1210 votes after a close canvass of the whole district, in parts of which he was well-known and had relatives.[6] I found that places which I had been obliged to leave practically unvisited such as Darraweit Guim and Bulla gave heavy majorities against me, but heavy general returns and an overwhelming miners' vote at Barry's Reef placed me that night nearly a hundred votes ahead of my opponent. For though he surpassed Cameron and in that night's returns totalled 1287, the Liberals brought up 1384 electors to vote for me. I was member for West Bourke.

[6] In March 1877 four candidates had stood for West Bourke. D. Cameron and J. T. Smith were returned, receiving 1210 and 1106 votes respectively.

4

'THE ABSOLUTELY UNEXPECTED CLIMAX'

Resignation, 1879

THE ELECTION FOR WEST BOURKE had attracted general attention owing to its occurrence at a critical hour, to the fact that there was just then a dearth of interesting events and to some extent to the circumstances of the struggle. In a few days it became famous everywhere and threatened to be historic. It was not till the second day after the election, while congratulations were still pouring in upon me from all quarters, that any importance was attached to the fact that the ballot papers at Newham were exhausted at 3.30 in the afternoon of polling day and that some persons were thus deprived of their votes. At first sight the incident seemed trivial because Newham itself was insignificant. An hotel and store, a post office and blacksmith's shop constituted the township and it was on the very border of the constituency, but it was a convenient centre for the western part of the well-settled Lancefield district, and a number of farmers found it more convenient than the larger townships. The local Deputy Returning Officer in consequence of the failure of ballot papers declared the poll postponed until the 22nd [February] when, he announced, the booth would be re-opened to continue the contest. If only those who had arrived too late on the 18th and who were apparently only four in number had been permitted to exercise the suffrage, or even if those who might ordinarily make it their centre or who were entered in the rolls as residents had been afforded another opportunity of voting, no interest would have been attached to the event; as with a lead of nearly one hundred votes without those already received at Newham, and of fifty-five after they were counted, there would have been no danger of my losing the seat. But there being only one roll containing 529 names of voters for the whole Lancefield district, though there were three polling places—Lancefield, Romsey and Newham—it was clearly possible if the contest

were renewed for both parties to bring up all they could of the
unpolled voters in the whole division, which stretched for miles
around. There was no real risk even then that the Conservatives
could have caught up some fifty votes, as only [   ]¹ votes remained
unrecorded including those of the dead, sick and absent. They could
at least have forced me to incur a considerable expenditure in addition to the £150 or so which I had spent already. The so-far defeated
party, however, saw their opportunity and became clamorous for
another day's polling. Ministers came rushing to me three-deep, full
of alarm. The Attorney-General, Sir Bryan O'Loghlen, pointed out
that there was no legal power to adjourn a poll except in the case of
a riot and that the proposal to re-open it because of a deficiency of
ballot papers would be illegal. Instantly all the dogs of party war
were yelping at his heels. The undoubted fact that some voters had
been disfranchised was seized upon and magnified until it was made
to appear that by the misadventure a seat had been lost to the Opposition and was now being fraudulently captured, against the will of
the electors, by and for the Ministry.

In a few days feeling was at a white heat. Ministers full of alarm
scurried to and from the *Age* office. The Opposition, full of rancour,
threatened to rouse the Colony.

An attempt was made to re-open the poll at Newham on the 22nd
when no scrutineer of mine was present and the rumour of it
reached Mr David Syme, who was spending the weekend as usual
at his country residence at Macedon. He at once rode across country,
entered the booth and in peremptory fashion forbade the returning
officer to commence until I was properly represented. He was surrounded by angry partisans and something like a scene ensued, of
which of course the most was made by the *Argus*. Eventually the
votes taken on the 18th were counted, totalling only 13 for me as
against 60 for my opponent. After this it was confidently assumed
that but for the failure of ballot papers Mr Harper would have been
successful and the whole Colony rang with plaints, taunts and bitter
outcries. As a matter of fact only four persons could be found who
had been deprived of their votes. At the next election six months
later [August 1879] when both parties strained every nerve to poll

¹ Blank in original.

well at this particular booth—I to make up numbers and he to justify
these complaints—the ballots were raised to 26 for me and 87 for
my opponent, a majority of 61 instead of 47 as on the first occasion.
If on February 18th he had polled the 87 and I had not gained
another vote beyond the 13 who supported me before 3.30 p.m.,
I should still have been the member. This was the largest majority
he ever gained here. After the rolls were swollen by the addition
of many who were not registered and eligible in February 1879 we
both gained, of course. Twelve months later [February 1880] my
total had risen to 44 and my opponent's to 94, sharing 138 voters at
Newham. After this the interest here began to decline. Six months
after [July 1880], 122 were polled (48 for me and 79 for him). Three
years later still, only 103 came to this booth, of whom 46 were my
supporters and 57 those of Mr Staughton. Never did the Conservatives obtain a sufficient majority here to have seated Mr Harper in
1879, though they polled specially at this booth in order to endeavour
to indicate as much for several succeeding elections. Though population if anything increased a little, the voters here in March 1883, in
1886 and in 1889 fell to the normal levels of [   ].[2]

Looking back, it is now proved beyond all question that I had
won the seat in February 1879, but at the time the mere doubt was
to me vexatious beyond expression. As soon as an appeal was made to
Sir Bryan O'Loghlen for a second day's poll, and before the votes
given were counted, I waited upon him to tender my resignation and
challenge another election over the whole district. I was full of fight
and eager to repeat a contest conducted under so many disadvantages,
and of whose issue with better opportunities of canvass I was in no
way afraid. The only objection was on the score of expense and
that I felt bound to face under such circumstances. Sir Bryan, however, courteously informed me that no return having been then made
by the Returning Officer, it was impossible to cancel what had been
done or order a new election. He dictated to me a protest against the
poll on the 22nd which I duly copied and handed to him.[3] After the
Newham votes were announced and the return published I again
repeated my offer, only to be once more informed that I had so far
nothing to resign. I was elected but would not be a member until

<hr>

[2] Blank in original.
[3] Reproduced, with other documents concerning the incident, in *Victoria, Parliamentary Debates*, xxx, 12-14.

sworn in, as I should be when Parliament met. I could receive no salary in the meantime and any recognition given to me was merely by courtesy and anticipation. There was no legal means of holding another election, even if I should die in the interim, until the writ had been returned to the Speaker when the House was sitting. Nevertheless I could not sit still when a war was being waged, so to speak, over my body. I remember attending one small but noisy meeting at Bacchus Marsh on March 1st, called to condemn the Ministerial action, where among the most prominent and hostile of opponents I first became acquainted with Mr S. T. Staughton.

In a week or two the excitement died away, though the incident was still cited as one of the many misdeeds of the Ministry and as an evidence of its tyrannous trampling upon the electors and the ballot box. But if it had done nothing else it had concentrated public attention upon the constituency, upon the curious contest, and upon myself as the innocent cause of so much angry feeling. Instead therefore of commencing as young members usually did, unknown outside the districts which had selected them, I was thrust into prominence before the whole Colony, enjoying notoriety of a not wholly pleasant character. My fellow members were curious to meet me and to secure me for public gatherings. Ministers took a paternal interest in their protégé though this did not lead them to fulfil the demands made upon them on my behalf by Mr Syme. Patterson at last tendered £50, professedly from his own pocket, which Mr Syme considered so inadequate that he supplemented it by £50 of his own on the grounds that, having undertaken at a moment's notice what was believed to be a hopeless fight to retain the seat for the Ministry when all older and more experienced politicians had declined the task, it was but fair that I should be recouped a part of my expenditure, especially as I could receive no salary as member until the House met six months later. Of course I declined both cheques with thanks, preferring to maintain my own independence of both Ministry and paper with whom as I foresaw I should some day have to part company, and determining therefore to be under no obligation of the kind to them or to anyone else. Needless to say I felt deeply grateful to Mr Syme and years afterwards did not forget Patterson's action, though made under pressure and for motives not wholly personal to myself.

The life of a member in recess was never idle and for the services

of a new member there were of course many extra demands. The
machinery of government is so much more extensive than in the old
world that Colonial constituents, continually brought into touch with
some of its departments, invoke the aid of their member with equal
frequency. West Bourke contained land in process of settlement and
of which the occupants were crown tenants; its shires were as eager
for grants from the Public Works Department as any others; it had its
fair share of dissatisfied school teachers, railway men and postmasters,
and the customary train of mechanics' institutes whose building and
book funds needed supplementing. All was, however, novel and amusing to me; so that weekly I escorted deputations to the public offices
or waited upon Ministers concerning their wants, and daily from a
dozen to a score of letters occupied my pen; while from one or two to
half a dozen interviews were required with aspirants for employment,
relatives of deceased or dismissed civil servants, and a miscellaneous
crowd of suitors associated with public movements or private
ventures desiring patronage, subscriptions, introductions, and advice
legal or constitutional but always gratis. Then there were the round
of local celebrations to be attended in the district in connection with
its shires, clubs, churches and institutes, meetings to be addressed,
and the constant efforts of opponents to make political capital out
of these forestalled, counteracted and overcome. To me these excur-
sions were for the most part picnics. I was beginning to make friends
and was hospitably welcomed in many places. Driving and riding
were pleasant pastimes and at Romsey in particular, where Stokes
dedicated a capital horse to my service, I had some delightful gallops
in his company. The town engagements soon became tedious but the
country expeditions were interesting and full of humorous sugges-
tion. To please the Institutes I prepared a lecture with the title
'How the People of England won their Reform Bill', in which I
endeavoured to give a spirited account of the Old Parliamentary
system with its rotten boroughs, and of the exciting events which
led up to the passage of the Reform Bill of 1832. There was no
allusion to local politics, but of course the parallel with the Reform
Bill which the Ministry were endeavouring to pass was suggested
at every step. It proved a success as lectures go, and was delivered
by me for the benefit of the various Associations right through the
district.

In all these expeditions I went alone and doubt if on a single

occasion I was ever accompanied by my colleague, Mr Donald
Cameron, whose acquaintance I did not make until some three
weeks after I had been returned and who was not unnaturally somewhat offended by being entirely ignored throughout the contest. We
met at a visit paid to Bacchus Marsh on March 6th [1879]. Afterwards
when I went to look him up I found him occupying a dirty little
upstairs room in Little Collins Street, containing a deal table, a
tumbled heap of newspapers and a few chairs. He earned his living
as Melbourne correspondent of some country papers to which he
also furnished leading articles of the usual type, altogether probably
receiving from £200 to £400 a year, according to the demand for
his services and the varying diligence with which he applied himself
to his task. As writer for the *Age* I looked down upon this new phase
of press life with pity and amazement, though he in his turn, I believe,
regarded me as from an even loftier eminence of authorship. His
heart was in his fiction of which he wrote a great deal that found
favourable acceptance in country papers, abounding as it did with
local colour, incident, and a certain strain of feeling which might
even be termed poetic. As at this time my own diet in fiction was
limited to George Eliot, Thackeray, Dickens, Victor Hugo, Haw-
thorne, and the classics (Fielding, Richardson and the like), my
admiration for his journalistic serials was always forced. We were
not entirely agreed about politics for he always relied on and hoped
to secure the Catholic vote, while his Protectionist principles
approached too nearly to Prohibition to please me. In all other respects,
in tastes, habits and opinions we were entirely unlike. He was a good-
looking man, above the middle height, with a well-shaped head and
well-cut features, aquiline in type and fair of hue. About forty years
old or a little more, he was already becoming bald, was careless in
his dress, and nervous in manner, oscillating between timidity and
aggressiveness. A pleasant and genial companion, he had not sufficient force of character, industry or self-control to acquire a leading
position; especially since as a rule he was a hesitating and ineffective
speaker even when well-prepared, and was almost helpless in sudden
emergencies. At first he was inclined to be somewhat haughty and
spiteful but this soon wore off before my happy indifference. Except
when introducing deputations or attending a Ministerial visit we
rarely met each other. In the constituency I went my own road
though of course always in friendliness to him. Lunching often at

Parliament House for the purpose, I gradually became familiar with most of the members and with Ministers, obtaining a good deal of insight into their methods and ideas in a conversational way. My association with the dreaded *Age* was a sufficient passport to their good graces and assured me much more consideration and respect than I should have otherwise obtained. The chief public appearance made by me was at Ballarat when Colonel Smith[4] addressed a crowded meeting of his constituents. My fiery and flamboyant speech was welcomed with immense applause and gave me a hopeful introduction to this great Liberal centre.

My Parliamentary debut was looked forward to by the party with considerable anticipations and I was allotted the honour of moving the Address when the next session opened on July 8th [1879]. By this time I was no novice in the everyday employments of a Member, was no stranger to most of those I addressed, and had enjoyed a good deal of experience in public speaking. Nevertheless like every beginner I was seized at once with a sense of the difference of facing men many of whom know more than yourself of the subjects upon which you speak, and all of whom are your superiors in experience of the Chamber. Always highly nervous no matter how small the gathering to which I spoke, on this occasion my condition was so agonizing as to seem to threaten mental paralysis. This was mitigated by the circumstance that I gave little or no indication of the tremors that thrilled me, dried my palate and robbed me of control of my voice and knowledge of my movements. The day had been one of torturing suspense and the afternoon was well-nigh unendurable. My admission was blocked by an Opposition protest against my being allowed to take my seat. Frenzied with apprehension, I sent for Mr Gaunson who was the active objector and confided to him my secret. At last I was allowed to enter, and sworn, but the refreshment hour had arrived and I was again postponed. I could neither eat nor drink but remained on the rack until able to deliver myself in some fashion of my carefully prepared speech, which closed with the absolutely unsuspected climax of my resignation and refusal to retain the seat upon an incomplete poll.[5]

4 William Collard Smith, M.P. for Ballarat West and Minister for Mines, had long been associated with the Volunteer Force, and was usually referred to by his military title, which in fact at this date was Major.

5 For the proceedings, and Deakin's speech, see *Victoria, Parliamentary Debates*, xxx, 12-31 (8 July 1879).

The situation has been described as one of the most dramatic witnessed in the House. The Opposition were complimentary; the Ministry silent and angry; their followers applauded wildly. I happened to ride home in the same omnibus with Berry who mildly remonstrated with me for taking such an action without consulting anyone. 'It's all very well for you,' said he, 'it puts you on a pinnacle. But what of the party if you lose them a seat at this juncture?' To say anything about principle before party seemed a futile and irrelevant answer to this very practical question put in his quietly emphatic way. I was not long allowed the pinnacle and soon learned that my action had been really dictated by all kinds of mean motives. As a fact I had endeavoured to resign in the first days after the discovery, but after the excitement had died away and I was everywhere received as member I thought little about the matter until I began to consider my future and to feel sensitive of entering the House with the slightest blot upon my escutcheon. Walking homewards through the Domain, when close to my old school, the sudden thought suggested itself—why not carry out my original intention as soon as ever I had the power; and I at once resolved to take a step which appealed alike to my sense of honour and my boyish feeling for a dramatic renunciation and defiance of my adversaries. From that instant I jealously locked my secret in my breast, sounding no one and hinting to no one what I meant to do. The effect counted upon was very partially realized even among my friends but quite sufficiently to satisfy me on that head, while the more I weighed it the more was I contented with what I had done. The speech in which I took such pride reads very poorly today. Its quotations from Spencer, Mill and Gladstone and crude dogmatism of the doctrinaire are but too apparent. It suffers also from the extreme rapidity with which it was uttered, its enunciation baffling all the reporters, except perhaps one, who attempted to take it down. His would be a very small part of the whole. It was not corrected by me afterwards and does not therefore as it stands allow its expression to be fairly judged. The House applauded it for its manner and its fire and its conclusion, and it was loudly hailed as a triumph by the party at the moment, and for some time afterwards afforded a standard of comparison for similar first speeches; but no doubt my extreme nervousness impaired its quality, while the haste of delivery destroyed its style so far as the report was concerned and it remains obviously a poor production.

In the contest which followed a month later, though introduced by a series of meetings at intervals almost from the date of delivery [of my speech in the House], I visited every corner of the constituency and spoke wherever even a small meeting could be secured. My friends were stimulated to the utmost. They at least felt their responsibility deepened by my action and accordingly I polled an additional 196 votes on August 22nd [1879] over my total of the previous February. But the Catholic vote this time went more solidly to the ballot box; and what was more effectual still the Conservatives had been busy in placing upon the roll at their own expense all the reliable voters whom they found to be unregistered, especially in the neighbourhood of Melbourne. We had taken no such action because no election was anticipated by my supporters and moreover we had no funds at our disposal. My opponent fought me with indomitable energy, with great ability, with all the power of the purse and all the influences of his party. His poll was 1608 votes, so that he won the seat from me by a majority of fifteen out of 3201. As two entries in my old diary next day remind me I had at the time no regret, was not dissatisfied with the election, but privately inscribed myself as 'well contented'—and so I have always remained.

5

'ELECTION PRANKS'

Episodes in Campaigning, 1879

M Y SUPPORTERS ON THE SECOND OCCASION indicated their sense of the personal sacrifice involved in my resignation by paying all the expenses of the contest except a few pounds. Of course under their management they were much less than on the preceding occasion. Very shortly after I accompanied Mr Sydney Watson, a squatter of the old colonial days, upon a trip to Fiji where he had certain undefined land claims or interests into which he wished to enquire. He paid my travelling expenses for the sake of my company; and a delightful trip it was to one like myself who had been nourished upon the glowing pictures of the tropics in *Westward Ho!*, *Locksley Hall*, *Enoch Arden* and similar pen pictures. The reality surpassed my imagination and enriched me with memories for many years after.

When I returned it was plain that a third contest was before me, as the general election was then approaching when I was selected with Cameron for the effort to capture the two seats for West Bourke. Before considering the political significance of this appeal to the country something may be said of the light-hearted and merry-tempered manners in which I was gaining experience as canvasser and public speaker. Insufferably tedious as the constant repetition of speeches upon the same topics thirty or forty times over must have been, the weariness was for the time concealed in my case by the practical jokes with which it was intermingled and the platform fencing for which it afforded frequent opportunities. So much was my power of repartee relied upon that my friends always made it a chief object to invite or challenge questioners or disputants to take the floor against me. Native quickness of thought, readiness of speech, enjoyment of humour and boyish irresponsibility combined with my now almost continuous experience in this kind of speaking to make me an adept when contrasted with the very imperfectly inform-ed storekeeper or farmer, who was often much against his will forced into sudden prominence and obliged for shame's sake to be pitted against the expert, with the certainty that in some way or other he would be made ridiculous. Such a duel is almost always very unequal and on unfair conditions to the hapless interrogator who is not much better protected even when he becomes an interjector. Easy triumphs of the kind redound little to the credit of the practised debater but increase his reputation greatly and also the size and liveliness of his meetings. Election times are always understood to permit a considerable degree of licence in these matters and certainly the number and variety of the pranks I played made my campaigns much merrier than any others of which I have had knowledge.

Finding that Mr Harper had a set speech which he always delivered as nearly as might be in the same order of treatment with the same illustrations and much the same expressions, I contrived to hear the greater part of it at Greendale; and then as I happened to be preceding him through Blackwood and on to the east I recast my own speech in the same form as his, followed the same order, perverting his illustrations to my own purposes and rounding off his arguments so as to set forth my own views. It was with indignation as well as consternation that he found himself everywhere being charged with stealing my speech and repeating my figures, besides afflicting his listeners with the tameness and sameness of a twice heard harangue.

I was scarcely more considerate to my own colleague who was industriously trimming to catch the Catholic vote by an evasive dealing with the question of paying the priests' schools according to the results obtained. My own views were pronounced, but in order not to prejudice him I contented myself with a simple announcement of the fact and made no aggressive attacks upon them. Whenever we were addressing a meeting in a strongly Catholic neighbourhood, however, I used to amuse myself and torment him by frequently recurring in the most unexpected way to the Education issue in some of its forms, occasionally with great apparent heat, until my unhappy colleague would almost slip from his chair with nervous anxiety lest I should break out in a declaration of war on behalf of the State Schools; thus making it inevitable for him either to support or oppose it. Then I would slip away to a new topic and just as he had regained his composure abruptly revert to the sore point and zigzag around it until his alarm became intolerable.

Nearly always he spoke first and had got his speech into good

order after a few meetings, when one night at a small place where
the risk might be safely taken I accepted his invitation to precede
him, and without any warning delivered his speech for him leaving
him to do the best he could with what was left of mine. Though
he was greatly perturbed the sting of necessity led him to make a
much better address than usual and to thoroughly enjoy the escapades
into which I was always plunging. Unfortunately I have no record
now either of the devices by which our Committees beguiled votes,
captured vehicles, turned their adversaries' horses loose the night
before polling, sprang surprises on each other's forces, polled doubtful votes, challenged the naturalization of the foreign born or the
age of young ratepayers. In the country districts horse-play of all
kinds was tolerated at election times and was certainly not discourag-
ed by me or by my associates, who, whatever their ages, most of
them entered heartily into all such devices.

I can only recall one or two of the many odd personal experiences
which were mine during these juvenile extravagances. The first,
typical of a number less dramatic, relates to a local oracle and ardent
opponent who like Cato 'gave his little Senate laws, and sat attentive
to his own applause'. A little better off and a little better informed
than his rustic neighbours, he was accustomed to dictate and dog-
matize to them especially upon public affairs without any better
acquaintance with them than he gained from a diligent reading of
the *Argus*. He was therefore informed upon only one side of each
question, but with this scanty store and a great deal of pomposity
contrived to impress himself even upon the Liberals and to become
the acknowledged leader of the Conservatives. He was a little man
with a rather weak voice, unimpressive manner and a slight drawl
which was supposed to point to aristocratic associations in his youth.
At the second or third election he attended one of my meetings carefully armed with a batch of *Argus*-made figures tending to show the
extravagance and incapacity of the Ministry in regard to their loan
moneys and general expenditure, then fiercely criticized on many
grounds. Naturally I was familiar with them all for I was constantly
writing replies to the *Argus* on these very points, my association
with the *Age* and *Leader* having been steadily on the increase. At
the close of my remarks he rose at the back of the Hall and with
evident nervousness stumbled through his figures designed to show
that Mr Berry had blundered badly in his handling of them. He put

his question, though rather tediously, quite plainly to me though probably to no one else. He was my chief adversary and an extremely bitter partisan and I felt that my revenge had come as, with the greatest possible politeness, deferring to him as a financial expert, I quoted a few of his figures out of order, adding another one or two also taken from the *Argus* but bearing on a different point to that which he had raised. Was this, I enquired, the question he wished to put?

After an interval he stammered 'No' and I hastened to proceed with more figures which he could also recognize as from the *Argus*, but not those he had selected, which I began interpreting in another manner with a casual enquiry as to whether that was the point to which he was directing the attention of the meeting. Every eye was on him, every ear hung upon his words; the silence was painful; my politeness was so unimpeachable that he could not be offended and yet he palpably felt his grip of the figures getting weaker and weaker. I was obviously trying to help him, he had remained standing and stared at all the time and could only mutter feebly a negative to my question.

Seeing that he was all but reduced to the requisite condition of confusion I once more with unfailing and inexhaustible patience and courtesy rapidly whirled and wove the different sets of figures in and out of each other with a deftness born of long practice, until he was evidently reduced to hopeless confusion. Once more I enquired if that was what he meant. Once more, and more timidly he gave an abashed 'No'. 'Then, Sir,' said I with the weary despair of a preceptor handling an utterly incompetent pupil, 'you are a financial expert. You are an authority on figures. Will you please tell this meeting yourself what you do mean? Tell it your own way. Never mind me. Tell the meeting what it is you do mean, if you mean anything or know anything at all about figures.' This sudden shock effectually banished his last remaining gleam of self-confidence. He stood trembling, tongue-tied, a picture of helpless imbecility. At last he sat down amid shrieks of laughter from all those over whom he had so long tyrannized with his tongue, slunk from the hall as soon as possible, and never appeared at an election meeting again. The punishment was cruel but he had been vindictive and malicious to the poorer men of the place who were not of his way of thinking, and probably deserved most of his humiliation.

Comparatively little violence has ever been offered or exhibited in my electoral campaigns. I have only been once actually threatened with an assault from a hot-tempered antagonist. It came to nothing then beyond a slight demonstration on his part; though while feeling ran as high as it did I was not infrequently threatened in an indirect way when bad blood and a heedless tongue were found in the same person. It meant nothing but an explosion of temper such as finds relief in swearing. My strongest supporters were mainly Scotch, with a few Irish from the north and an odd Catholic or two who dared to defy priest and neighbour. The English were rarely active, though staunch, and remained undemonstrative or were but quiet workers. My pronounced antagonism to the Catholic claims set almost the whole of the Irish of that denomination against me. At a meeting in Keilor, one of their centres, the room in which I was speaking was long and narrow, having at the far end one or two windows, with sills three feet or so from the ground, which were lifted as high as they would go as the room was hot and close.

On one of the sills, dangling his legs, sat an irrepressible Pat who persisted in his interjections during my speech without much regard to their relevancy, and refused to be quieted, though often expostulated with by those near to him. It was my invariable practice never to ask or allow these disturbers to be interfered with by the policeman who was present, or indeed by anyone else. They did not injure me but either gave me opportunities to score at their expense or roused the feelings of my friends and stimulated their energies. In this case the unexpected happened, for while the interjector was uttering one of his unseasonable yells the next man to him suddenly swung round the back of his hand, taking the bawler right on the jaw so that his heels flew up and he vanished head downwards into the adjacent garden where it is to be presumed he found a soft resting place; for the striker promptly drew down the window and leaned against it serenely while the disturber was heard and seen no more.

In Bulla, another stronghold of the Catholics, I always polled well because there happened to be a deadly clan feud among them by which they were almost evenly divided. The fact that one party of them supported Harper was in itself sufficient to render the other party devoted adherents of mine. One evening on which I was addressing them in the local Shire Hall began and continued as peacefully as usual, though I had been warned that the rival factions were both strongly represented and that I must be prepared for squalls. As this was of necessity my general condition it made no difference to me or my address. All the seats before me were filled while a number of men were standing, some of them near the benches, others leaning against the walls. There was nothing done or said by me out of the ordinary procedure nor apparently was I a factor in the case, unless the applause or dissent awarded to me aggravated one party or the other. All I knew was that suddenly a man moved from one side of the hall to the back and without any word that I could hear struck one of those quietly lounging there a sounding blow in the face. He at once hit back; one or two others promptly sprang forward; and in an instant the whole of the rear of the hall was a confused mass of men, a few fighting and others trying either to separate them, or to secure them a fair field, or withdraw from the scene of strife.

After a moment or two of confusion while I stood patiently waiting for the broil and the tempest of clamour which attended and surrounded it to subside, one of the handsomest young fellows I have ever seen, curly-headed, bright-eyed, well-featured and finely limbed, rose from his seat and stepped quietly across the hall; his hands still at his sides and an expression of nonchalant sweetness on his face. Arrived at the swaying throng in conflict he suddenly lifted and shot out a great fist which struck one of the combatants in the face and felled him in his tracks. Another step, another blow, and a second was floored as cleanly and decisively. A third step, a third lightning spring of the arm, and the third went down as cleanly and as hopelessly as his fellows. That finished the fray. He still advanced as quietly and composedly as before but his opponents no longer waited to face him but fled outside, those he had knocked down following as fast as they could. He dawdled through the door after them and sounds indicated that he was chasing them once or twice around the hall, until they took to their heels and I resumed my remarks without taking any notice of the interruption. Presently the young hero who fortunately for us happened to be a supporter, entered as modestly and to all appearances as unbreathed and composed as when he first rose to perform his brilliant piece of pugilism. That was the only real disturbance I ever witnessed at an election, but I was once an actor in a scene of more serious nature still.

E

The miners at Barry's Reef, mainly Cornishmen closely united in religious belief and political principles, were accustomed to act together in almost a communal way. They were the staunchest of Liberals and very fiery in their enthusiasm. At the second contest, following my resignation, they were greatly incensed by the threatened falling away of a storekeeper and a few others who usually were of their way of thinking, under the blandishments of a political agent sent up by the Conservatives with plenty of money in his pocket to treat those whom he might possibly induce to support Mr Harper. Such a man was unknown in Blackwood and the unconcealed attempt at bribery was deeply resented as an imputation upon their honesty. That night the Mechanics' Institute was filled as usual, every form carrying its close set rank of stalwarts or sturdy miners, clean, patient, attentive as if in chapel, and as deeply in earnest. Then entered with a jaunty air, well-dressed, spick-and-span, a fresh-coloured man somewhat in sporting style and with an impudent assurance that was almost a swagger taking his seat rather forward of the centre. The meeting began as was customary and I was soon launched into my speech; and by the time I was half through I was as usual speaking with great impetuosity and fire, followed as always here with a growing accompaniment of cheers and stamping as the audience became more and more excited. Suddenly and without warning I contrasted with the simple upright elector relying upon his reason and his vote to give effect to his principles, to secure just laws and to protect his rights against invasion, the man who put all these in peril, seeking either to rob him of the effect of his vote or what was worse to tempt him and others to barter their birth-right for a mess of pottage, and the future of their families and their country for beer. The man at whom and of whom I spoke cowered as well he might at the thunders of applause that followed this as I pursued the line of thought further, asking what cause it was which found it necessary to bribe to secure votes and what kind of creature destitute of manliness, conscience and patriotism they discovered willing to stoop to the degrading work of temptation, subornation and treachery. I was quivering with excitement myself and the whole crowd appeared to be quivering too as they answered my appeals, no longer with applause but with a low, threatening, increasing and ominous growl.

Then my breath almost stopped. Scores of gleaming eyes and

vengeful faces were fixed upon mine and turning angrily towards
the man in the midst who crouched lower and lower before the
approaching storm evidently about to burst upon his devoted head.
There was no more jauntiness or impudence now. He was as white
as a sheet, and trembling as a sail does when a boat is going about.
It needed only a few more words and a gesture and what would
have been left of him when he escaped from those sinewy arms would
probably have been unrecognizable. When my heart beat again, as
it seemed after a pause as long as eternity, I realized for the first
time what I was doing, that I must not stop but must lead the
lightning generated to strike elsewhere. Without a perceptible halt
therefore I continued as if in the same vein a furious denunciation
of the classes who employed such agents, their past history, their
present plans, their financial hold upon the country and how it might
be saved from their grasp; so gradually winding away from the man
and his mission until they were occupied with other questions and
forgot him. Never have I passed so dreadful a quarter of an hour
as that; and as for the man, I only know that he rose with the first
to leave and melted into the night. An hour afterwards at my hotel
he furtively entered my room still pallid and unnerved and seizing my hand said, 'Sir, you saved my life tonight and I know it.
By God, Sir! You saved my life and I shall never forget it. I will
never act against you again.' So far as I know he never did and for
my part I never repeated my dangerous experiment. But the ten
votes which he caused to change sides at Barry's Reef in that election cost me the seat. Nor have I regretted that either. I escaped a
tedious tariff session in which I should have been most unhappy,
as I was in all tariff sessions since. The probabilities are that I should
have become embroiled with the ministry and have formed entangl-
ing alliances. And then I should have lost the delightful trip to Fiji.

6

'BEGINNING TO BE SOBERED'

Defeat and Victory, 1880

THE GENERAL ELECTION OF FEBRUARY 1880 began under omens very unfavourable to the Ministry and reflecting upon all their supporters. Ministers individually had been guilty of blunders worse than crimes, of jobberies not serious in themselves but, what was electorally worse, ridiculous; and most fatal of all were clearly convicted of having held office during a series of bad seasons which had depleted the revenue, aggravated all rural interests, compelled them to impose fresh taxation and confused their programme of legislation. Their general record, taking into account the bad times, was by no means discreditable and they had accomplished much vigorous administration; but the good impression they ought to have made was marred by want of coherence, reticence and dignity in their public acts and speeches. They had been wearied by guerrilla tactics in Parliament and violent abuse out of it into imprudencies which came home to roost when they faced the country somewhat out of heart and with an Opposition as keen, relentless, and in the Press as unscrupulous, as ever existed in Victorian politics. The Catholics were up in arms against them, and the farmers were alarmed; nor did the quality of their candidates bear favourable comparison as a rule with those of their Conservative rivals. Above all the *Age*, partly from discontent because its doctrinaire programme was not adopted wholesale by Berry, partly from disgust at the Ministerial escapades, and partly from jealousy of the Premier's commanding influence in the country, lent but a critical support to the Government; coquetting with a disaffected section of their followers headed by Mr Munro and Mr Casey and more than hinting that a reconstruction of the Cabinet was necessary if it was to retain public confidence. The Ministry fought well, and considering their allies and opponents, did well, but their majority vanished and they resigned office before meeting Parliament.

As was natural in a writer for the *Age* I was as a candidate myself considerably out of sympathy with the Ministry and its policy. In some points I had always been independent. In my first election I had at once separated myself from them in regard to their injustice to the dismissed public servants and was unable to endorse the basis of their land tax. After six months' experience of membership I distinguished my position still more clearly by opposing some of the increases of Protective duties which they were proposing and by rejecting their proposal for a Nominee Upper House. These were two of the main planks of their platform and my attitude upon both was so independent that one of the Ministerial papers contended that at my second election I had little more reason for being classed as a supporter of the Government than as a member of the Opposition. In consequence of this and similar reflections, and to insist upon my freedom of action and to avoid any possible misunderstanding prior to entering upon a third campaign, I wrote to the Bacchus Marsh Branch of the Reform League, then the most active and influential Liberal organization in the constituency, a letter which was duly published in the *Bacchus Marsh Express* plainly stating my antagonism to anything like Prohibition and generally asserting my independence of the details of the Ministerial policy, with whose general scope and character I was in accord. The step illustrates at once the freedom which I claimed and the indifference I felt as to whether I was to become a candidate for West Bourke or not. I was in no hurry to be a member and cherished the comfortable conviction that I could reach the House as soon as I wished by several roads. Some overtures were made to me from South Gippsland and other parts but if possible it was my ambition to win this difficult seat. The personal rivalry between Mr Harper and myself was becoming intensified and providing I was left a sufficiently free hand in regard to my programme I was anxious for a fight to a finish as between us. My terms were accepted by the Reform League of the district, and Cameron and myself nominated against Messrs Harper and Staughton for the two seats.

The task before us was not easy. A great deal of money and energy were spent on the election generally and particularly in West Bourke because of the notoriety it had gained. We had through the Leagues enrolled what friends we could but our efforts were relatively ineffectual against the systematic work done steadily by our opponents, owing to their superior resources. I addressed thirty meetings in

almost a fortnight and canvassed hard. Blackwood did well for us,
giving me 184 and Cameron 172 to Harper's 27 and Staughton's
25. They gained on us a little generally through the country where
the Catholic vote was most marked, as at Romsey, but it was in the
suburbs, Essendon and Flemington, that they drew away from us
and won both seats; Harper heading the poll with 1942 votes,
Staughton following with 1889, beating my 1876 by only 13 votes and
Cameron's 1739 by 150 [28 February 1880]. Taking into account
the odds against us it is surprising that we did so well. My three totals
were 1397, 1593 and 1876, a marked advance each time; but [Harper's]
were 1342, 1608 and 1942, a still more remarkable record. Cameron
had marched from 1210 to 1739, in itself a great poll. On both sides
the party discipline was excellent and certainly the defeat was not
a disgrace. Our expenses were paid for us by our loyal adherents
and once more I took my beating quietly, though this time philo-
sophically rather than with the recognition that it was for the
best with which I had welcomed my earlier overthrow. It seemed
certain then that for two or three years at least the political door
was closed upon me, and upon West Bourke probably forever.

I was beginning to be sobered. As the electioneering lost its novelty
it lost its attractions. The day of jests and pranks was drawing to a
close and it was clear that if I again entered the political arena it
must be more seriously and with a graver sense of responsibility. My
press work had increased until it occupied almost the whole of my
time and I was paid on the highest scale then reigning. In every
respect my position was more assured. Manhood naturally meant
more circumspection and I not unnaturally began to turn my thoughts
to provision for my future. But despite my intended renunciation
of political activity I was soon brought into the field again and once
more in conspicuous fashion.

When the Service Reform Bill was introduced [20 May 1880]
it was determined to hold a mass meeting in Melbourne in order
to give the Opposition cue to the country, and that no Members
should be asked to address it. By some chance the first place on the
programme was given to me. The Bill had been just circulated and
I had but a few hours to study it and form my conclusions. I analysed
it to the best of my ability and in a state of pitiable nervousness crept
to the Princess Theatre where a sight met my astonished gaze that
fairly took my breath away. A packed crowd some 2500 strong,

obviously in a high state of emotional tension, crammed every corner
of the old building and when, after a few random remarks from a
rough chairman, I was called upon to make my first important speech
to a Melbourne mass meeting, familiar as I had become with audiences
up to 300 or 400 strong, I was almost paralysed into speechlessness. Nor
was my misery lessened by the cries of disapprobation which my
first compliments to the Liberal parts of the measure provoked from
too ardent partisans. I nevertheless kept firmly on my way. My
exposition was listened to with the most marked curiosity chiefly
because the Bill was not yet understood by the public and in part
because of my past contests. When at last, having prepared my hearers
to appreciate the critical features of the scheme, I commenced to
strike hard, the meeting followed me eagerly, saluted every point
with rounds of applause and at the conclusion accorded me an
immense ovation. My position as a public speaker was at once established. Not only was the address the speech of the evening, but as it
supplied a good deal of information not up till then available, gave
in a sense the keynote to the critics of our party in the press and elsewhere throughout the country.[1] The Bill so far as we were concerned
was condemned in advance before it had been considered at all in
the House and at the same time my name was associated with it
as one of the leaders of the Liberal Opposition. One consequence was
another call from West Bourke to represent them, and another a
certain party prominence possessed by no one else outside Parliament
except Vale.

Meanwhile the Service Government of 1880 was going to its doom.
It was sufficiently strong in personnel though degraded by the inclusion of Mr Bent, whose services to his party, though mainly of a kind
little creditable to either, had been so useful, and whose loyalty
to it was so obviously mercenary, that it was not considered safe to
pass him over. The smallness of the Ministerial majority was largely
responsible for his inclusion, while a faint hope of appeasing the
Catholic antagonism to Service led to the appointment of Mr John
Duffy. Bent's vulgarities and ineradicable tendencies to jobbery soon
injured the prestige of the Cabinet while O'Shanassy's influence with
the Church was far too great to be counter-balanced by Duffy. There
was the usual proportion of political rats like H. R. Williams, who

[1] This meeting was held on 28 May 1880.

having deserted the Berry Ministry without finding a place with their successors now prepared to desert them too; and Graves whose vote up to the very last hour was left in uncertainty. Service himself as the critical division on the Reform Bill approached went to the corner and sitting beside Graves frankly asked him where he intended to sit in the forthcoming [division]. With a grin of nervous anxiety he replied, 'I don't know. I have not yet made up my mind.' The disgust which the Premier felt at this avowal was too deep to be concealed, but as he rose to leave the trimmer without another word, Graves laid a detaining hand upon his arm and with a fiendish chuckle of amused self-contempt whispered in his ear, 'Ain't I a b——r!' and fell back in his seat full of admiration of his own inconstancy. The chief blow to the Reform Bill upon which the Ministry had staked its fortunes came not from creatures like these but from Wrixon, whose constitutional principles fortified under Higinbotham were shocked by the proposal to admit the Legislative Council to a share in the financial powers properly belonging to the Assembly alone. After a night of great excitement on June 25 [1880] upon which I looked from the Gallery, the Bill was defeated by two votes. On June 29 a House of four months old was dissolved.

The common cry has been that in so acting Service committed an unpardonable blunder on the ground that he ought to have retained office and after a time submitted another Bill. It is very doubtful if he would have been allowed the opportunity but in any case the course he followed was the more dignified exit and promised, if successful, to have ruined the Liberal Party and broken its power for some years to come. Had he consented to come to an understanding with the Catholics he could have carried the country which we faced with an irregular and motley crew of candidates, with empty purses, dispirited by reverses and needing but a sharp blow to split into fragments. The dissolution was daring but the crisis demanded nothing less. The colony was weary of the long agitation for reform, the turn in the financial tide was coming, ushering in a series of good seasons, and what was peremptorily necessary in the public interest was peace.

Sir Bryan O'Loghlen who had lost his seat for West Melbourne consented to contest West Bourke with me and this again assisted to rivet general attention upon that constituency. He took his part in the fray as calmly and lethargically as usual, with unruffled good temper and politeness. The bulk of the platform work and canvassing fell to me, and upon me was consequently concentrated the fiercest fire from the press of our opponents. This time there was but little relief in the way of practical jokes to the hard work of the campaign. The electors were weary and so were we, though realizing the final character of the struggle I flung myself into it with desperate determination. O'Loghlen's name proved sufficiently effective, quite as much by reducing the poll for our opponents as by increasing ours. At Keilor and Bulla I only rose from 37 to 41 and from 72 to 88, and at Darraweit Guim from 14 to 23; while Harper fell from 77 to 71, from 57 to 33, and from 45 to 37 at these Catholic centres. The increments were small but they sufficed; for I headed the poll with 1906 votes, Sir Bryan following with 1873, Staughton taking third place with 1772, and Harper coming last with 1742. Last time he was 66 above me, this time 164 below. After this he abandoned the constituency, and no wonder.

Never in Victoria or in any other colony had there been four closely contested, costly and bitter elections fought within eighteen months in the same constituency, in each instance between the same men. The results had accurately represented the feeling of the colony at the time, and hence their importance. [Harper's] drop from the 1942 votes of February 1880 was exactly 200. My poll showed a steady advance each time, beginning with 1397, going on to 1593, then to 1876 and finally to 1906. No doubt the Catholic vote just turned the scale though with it O'Loghlen only polled 134 more votes than Cameron did almost without any of it, and I had only grown by 30 votes with all its aid. It was always a difficult factor to trace and even when most distinctly challenged as in this election its operation was by no means clear. It is quite possible that all we got of it was due to the Irish feeling of some of the electors who preferred to follow O'Loghlen rather than their priests, and that those who were Catholics first continued to vote against me. In the country the general result was much the same. The narrow Ministerial majority disappeared and left the Liberals, without Sir John O'Shanassy, in a small majority; so that it was plain that the situation was still unstable. But it was equally plain that the House now chosen could not be disposed of as summarily as its predecessor and that it must in some way settle the great question of the hour. Under such circumstances I once more became a Member of Parliament.

At this point, perhaps, a momentary digression of a strictly personal character may be permitted without reproach, as demanded by the nature of these sketches, something in the nature of a soliloquy made as an aside. At the outset of my career I resembled only too well most young men of my age in that so far as I had any definite ambition at all it was for a life of literary fame and exercise. Journalism did me one service in teaching me how laborious such a career must be, how poorly paid in cash and how great or singular a capacity it required to establish a reputation or achieve anything commensurate with the sacrifices and toil it demanded. By no means an idler and endowed with a considerable share of restless energy, I was yet quite unprepared for the close, patient, unremitting, minute, consistent and cumulative application demanded of all aspirants for such honours. Like most youths I was not mercenary, having indeed a profound distaste for business and a disdain of the monotonous regularities and pettinesses of the habits it required. A modest competence was all I asked—£300 to £500 a year marking the range within which I should have felt myself content. Even this was hoped for as a consequence of work done for its own sake and without an immediate aim at financial results. Bargaining of any kind, haggling for a profit, the endeavour to leave the other party to the transaction a loss, or to pick his pocket by superior knowledge, skill, or situation seemed to my romantic mood a disagreeable as well as doubtfully honest procedure. The influence of trade wholesale or retail, but especially the latter, seemed to my adolescence as to the ancient Greeks unworthy of a free man and inconsistent with independence. I was therefore entirely repelled from any employment directly associated with the making of money.

Journalism had gratified, amused, rewarded but disgusted me. Its constant concern with those transient occurrences and the superficial aspects of current affairs which constituted the mass of its subject matter from day to day seemed but little more honourable than the glaring selfishness of commercial life. Then again the narrowness of partisanship, the restrictions imposed by association with partisans only and the subordination of all views to those deemed best for the paper and its party threatened to suffocate one's own opinions, reducing the mind to a machine and one's pen to that of a press hack. These considerations drew me into public life where again I was doomed to find myself fettered so soon as I exhausted the freshness and interest which belonged to a new field. It took me some years before I became able to assert whatever individuality there was in me, under conditions to which I must presently refer. At the outset however I felt myself a bird of passage still.

I had earned my living by teaching until I hated the drudgery of the class work with its endless repetitions, having at that time no appreciation and probably at no time the power of seizing the golden opportunities of developing the young by which the true teacher can elevate his task to the highest. Between my scholastic essays I had represented my father's money in a manufacturing business, acting for some two years as a bookkeeper and financial manager until I loathed the dreary pursuit of £s.d. as much as if all its gains were losses. Journalism though preferable at first was soon seen to lead to an almost equally mechanical mode of earning one's living. Men of more ability might have been able here, as in my previous pursuits, to assert themselves and rise above their environment but to me it seemed that whatever thin thread of individual ability I possessed must soon be worn away in these walks of life. Public life afforded a broader field but that too my own narrowness threatened to make too narrow. So it came about that for a long time I engaged in it with but half a heart, having many distractions and many other tastes.

Better acquaintance with the theatre had destroyed my boyish ambition to become an actor though this had filled me for years. A more extended knowledge of the drama destroyed the companion idea, still longer cherished, that I could write as well as perform poetic plays on the Shakespearian model. The growth of judgment next satisfied me that the poetry so long loved and its production practised in secret for many years, was too poor by comparison with that of even the minor singers to be worthy of preservation. Finally my hope of doing anything permanent in prose died gradually away. The platform to which I then turned with the idea of preparing and delivering essays upon literary, social and religious issues from an open unsectarian Sunday pulpit also proved to be above my reach. Every aim which I had pursued was thus abandoned until my faculty such as it was ran into the mould furnished by my environment. So it was that at length I became a politician from 1880 till 1890 by sheer force of circumstance rather than independent choice.

A knowledge of these various purposes and attachments of mine may throw light upon the part I afterwards played but its relevancy lies in its relation to the views of men and movements here expressed. I have always remained so-to-speak detached from my associates and from my own public pursuits by a love of study which has sent me into solitude instead of into society, and a felicitous home life which has caused me to shrink still more from many of the functions and festivities of members of Parliament. Few men actively engaged in politics have lived so much apart or dabbled during their public careers in so great a variety of foreign enquiries and interests. In fine the life I have actually lived, though on the whole hugely enjoyed, has only by degrees become congenial to me and has only been accepted reluctantly when door after door which I should have preferred to open proved beyond my power to unbar. My ideal has always been to live far from towns though actually born, bred and always confined to them, travelling for a few years in an unpretentious way and afterwards earning by my pen a small sufficiency by the publishing of the very best that thought, observation and study should enable my mind to yield to the cause of culture. To have spent my days in retirement without public appearances, public speaking or public notice under a veil of anonymity and largely in communion with Nature, and with my inner self in the presence of Nature, represents the dream cherished by me with but slight alteration from boyhood up to the hour of writing. It is unnecessary to add that this being denied I am far more than content for myself with the path I have been obliged to follow, which I retrace in memory not only without bitterness but with gratitude.

With this outline of myself as seen by myself the reader should be able to some extent to understand the standpoint occupied by me and can allow for it in judging my description of the scenes in which I was an actor. The very nature of these papers dealing as they attempt to do only with the inner and as yet unwritten side of public life, renders them apparently a *chronique scandaleuse* though as a matter of fact everything relating to the private life of my associates is scrupulously ignored. The private aspect of public life so far as it appears worth noting is here attempted to be fairly set down, as it may be without any breach of confidence, for the information of those curious as to the real manner of conducting the affairs of a Colony prior to the Federal Union. Up to this point I have told my story without quotation from newspapers or documents and almost entirely without reference to them. The general political evolution of the times is not sought to be explained, and even the fortunes of its party campaigns are but lightly and vaguely sketched as a background. It has not seemed necessary to add to my reminiscences any of the reports of my speeches or articles which might have been cited in a more pretentious chronicle. The aim of these chapters is to add to these public records which are and will be always available to every enquirer a supplementary memoir which may be hereafter serviceable in assisting the interpretation of Victorian political developments, often much misunderstood at the time and generally misconstrued since. Rusden's *History*[2] for instance is as untrustworthy as a partisan pamphlet well can be without deliberate dishonesty, while the *Argus* and *Age* accounts are alike perverted by reckless partisanship. The *Argus* papers on Parliament, 'Above the Speaker', written by Willoughby, are masterpieces of consistent and deliberate misrepresentation . . . I shall continue to include here only those items which are not fully or perhaps at all given anywhere in print. This, I repeat again, is not a history but a collection of some further materials for a history not to be found in Hansard or the newspapers, if ever the future requires that one should be written. It is a purely personal series of recollections, without authority, and requiring like all such private memoranda to be checked most carefully; though as far as I can make it it is conscientious and unbiassed, though of course incomplete.

---

[2] *History of Australia*, by G. W. Rusden (1819-1903), (Melbourne, 3 vols., first edition 1883, second edition 1897). Rusden was Clerk of the Victorian Legislative Council, 1856-81.

7

'A COURSE OF MY OWN'

The Reform Bill, 1880-1

COALITIONS HAVE BEEN BLESSED or banned in the abstract from several standpoints though surely no question can be less determinable by principle, or more dependent upon time, place and circumstances. In the rudimentary Parliamentary life of young countries they are often unavoidable and not infrequently highly advantageous. Even when most to be desired, they are not always possible for personal or ethical reasons. It is doubtful if Berry at the head of his overwhelming majority in 1877 would have allowed Service more than a single colleague, with perhaps another ally in the Council without office, and it is questionable whether Service could have been reasonably expected to enter a Cabinet in which he was to be so outnumbered by men from whom he was separated by considerable differences. Nevertheless Service and Casey could have done much, and if it had been possible to enrol Francis too instead of Longmore, Lalor and Woods, a powerful but temperate and widely influential Cabinet could have been secured while much delay, bitterness and misbehaviour would have been avoided. Grant and Patterson could have been relied upon to catch the prevailing tone while Berry and Smith needed only such judicious counsellors to have advanced by more pacific and tactful ways towards the same ends as those which they pursued, when alone, through strife and turmoil. It is but too probable however that the antagonisms between the men named were too wide to render them then capable of efficient cooperation.

In 1880 the situation had entirely altered and was ripe for such a union. The high handed policy of 1877-9 had failed to coerce the Council and the Service attempt to reform it had been rejected in its turn. What more natural than that the moderates on each side should combine to improve upon the last proposals so as to secure a reasonable reform without further conflict? This was the course actually pursued, but in an unsatisfactory way. That a coalition of some kind was inevitable between parties so evenly balanced was conclusively proved a year later. The very first steps I took as a Member sought to bring about an honourable union of parties. They were afterwards justified most amply by our experiences, but the astonishing thing is that I should have been able to take any part at all in so important and vital an issue within two or three days of my being sworn in. As a matter of fact I took the chief part in the negotiations for the Liberal party, a good deal on my own initiative, but with the consent of Mr Berry who was prepared to rate my capacities far higher than I did myself, and who treated me from the outset as if I was already in the front rank. The effect of the four contests for West Bourke and of the place awarded to me as a platform speaker, together with my association with the editorial staff of the *Age*, combined to thrust me into a prominence which in this particular association I was quite content to occupy and use, but from which I at once shrank as soon as the parley was over. Whatever my faults at this time may have been I was by no means anxious to rush to the front in Parliament, being quite satisfied in my own mind that there was a long apprenticeship to serve before I should be fitted to assume greater responsibilities than those of the average member. For a few days however my position was remarkable and the whole situation unique.

The formal votes by which the Service Ministry were displaced accounted for 84 out of 86 members, reckoning the Speaker, 35 supporting and 48 opposing them. Two of the Opposition were absent so that their majority was actually 15. This total included the Catholic party which at its full strength was about nine strong, more than sufficient to turn the scale without reckoning the four or five Ministerialists who were in sympathy with them. It was rendered less effective because its leadership might at any moment be divided, more than half of them as Liberals looking to O'Loghlen while the remainder, though they cannot be said to have preferred O'Shanassy, submitted to his predominance in ability and experience. The genial, gentle, indolent, lethargic, procrastinating, improvident and impoverished Baronet was as manifestly his rival's superior by birth, breeding and education as he was his inferior in strength of will and character and intellect. Physically a giant, with a splendid head and rugged features of proportionate dimensions, O'Shanassy was the

peasant in build, gait and habit though lifted by his life's training
and brain-power as clear of his compatriots of the same class as was
Burns by his genius. He had passed through his radical stage in the
early days of the colony when he earned a reputation for leadership,
discounted by a disposition to jobbery in the interests of his country-
men and a marked subservience to his Church. His jealousy of
[Charles Gavan] Duffy, a later arrival, was only less marked than
Duffy's jealousy of him but his pigheaded obstinacy and master-
fulness at that time quite overcame the subtlety, finesse and insincer-
ity[1] of his more brilliant competitor. Duffy was liberal by instinct
and on reflection, and remained true to his colours to the last.
O'Shanassy, who had acquired his political knowledge as he acquired
his business knowledge, by hard experience, went on to build up
a considerable fortune and becoming a large landholder became in
all good faith (as was natural to a man of his type) steadily more
Conservative. Excluded from politics, he read judiciously and continued to observe with keen-sighted practical eye the progress of
affairs and to deduce his conclusions from what he saw.

At this time, after a period of comparative quiescence in the Legislative Council, he had returned to the Assembly an elderly but still
vigorous man, a true Parliamentarian familiar with constitutional
principles and full-freighted with its precedents; of great administra-
tive ability and of constructive power in legislation, a weighty and
dignified speaker, only excluded from the highest offices of the state
by his devotion to his creed and his determination to secure for its
priestly schools a sufficient subsidy from the state exchequer. On
the other hand exclusion from office had rendered his never patient
temper very peevish and had stimulated an ungovernable appetite
for power into a reckless rage for mastery very ill-concealed. He was
an accomplished though impatient intriguer, somewhat uncouth
in manner and unwieldy in bulk but bold, resolute and firm, unflinch-
ing in defeat, arrogant in victory and truculent when brought to bay.
A stern strong man, he stood in mind as in body head and shoulders
above the great majority of his associates. At this time he looked
forward to an alliance with Berry, cherishing wild dreams of the
Premiership but considering the Chief Secretaryship and co-equal
authority within his grasp and the ultimate control of the Ministry
not far beyond. His one condition as to policy was the immediate

---

[1] So in MS., despite the next sentence.

Sir John O'Shanassy

granting of a Commission of Enquiry into the Education question and he had marked out in his mind two colleagues in the Council, one with a portfolio and one without. With O'Loghlen as Attorney-General one half of the Cabinet would then have been Catholic in policy.

O'Loghlen, on the other hand, not unwilling to accept this position, was hurt that there should be doubt or delay in acceding to this plan. The last two elections had made the influence of the Catholics at the polls in his opinion paramount so that he could no longer as of old postpone their claims for school grants as inopportune. He felt the danger of allowing O'Shanassy to monopolize the confidence and support of the Church while as the leader of the Clare clan he nourished a mildly persistent antagonism to the chieftain of their Tipperary rivals. At this time too the increasing moderation of Berry's programme displeased him. He had been out of Parliament for six months and had not been softened by that privation. In his quietly obstinate way he had determined that he would require when re-accepting the Attorney-Generalship, for which he saw no rival in the field, the same condition as O'Shanassy whether the latter joined or not. The two were therefore acting together and yet not entirely in harmony, each looking forward to the possible exclusion of the other, and both prepared to make terms independently if need be, though both pledged to insist upon some express recognition of the Catholic claims. Since 1872 almost the whole of their electors and representatives had made this the one supreme end of their politics, having steadily sought to eject Ministry after Ministry in the hope of one day finding a government sufficiently weak to purchase their aid. It now seemed to them that their hour had come. The gulf between Liberals and Conservatives had been deepened until it appeared impassable, while the votes which could be counted upon to support the denominational grant ranged from a certain fifteen to a possible five-and-twenty. The situation was plain to others as well as themselves and the *Age*, then as always staunch for a strictly secular educational system, boldly declared for a coalition. It was therefore in harmony with its aim that Berry cast about him for a compensating alliance which should enable him to dispense with the Catholic section altogether. One man and one man alone possessed the key to the position, and this was Wrixon.

Irish too, but of a Protestant family and like O'Loghlen a Dublin

F

University man and barrister, he had practised with some considerable success, especially in the western circuit, until marriage with
a wealthy widow relieved him of the necessity of following his profession further. Trained in politics under Higinbotham, his senior
colleague and model, he was as far removed from the everyday
world and as little in touch with the average man as his master; like
him refined in disposition and studious in habit, but with a far less
commanding presence and far less motive power of will. A frank and
upright gentleman, greatly the superior of O'Loghlen in flexibility
of mind and grace of oratory and as much superior to O'Shanassy
as he was in culture, in bearing and in good taste, he was no more
a match for the old lion than the Baronet. He would face him fear-
lessly in debate but against his strenuous dogmatic dominance could
offer no more effectual bar than trains of reasoning somewhat too
fine-drawn, and appeals to higher considerations which by contrast
with the strong sense of O'Shanassy appeared merely scholarly and
utopian. To this loveable and entirely trustworthy man, independent
in views as in fortune and animated by the sincerest and most
unselfish desire to serve his country, it now became my curious lot
to appeal on behalf of a coalition between Berry and himself, which
adopting a moderate policy should put both O'Shanassy and
O'Loghlen with their following severely on one side.

Accordingly I visited him at his private residence in Kew, an
accredited emissary from Syme and Berry, to find him perfectly
willing to enter into the proposed alliance if he could do so honour-
ably with the consent and support of those among his party with
whom he thought he ought to act. Separated from them by his
opposition to the Service Reform Bill he had, now that the Ministry
was practically ejected from office, no reason why he should not rejoin
them and indeed he had acted with them and against Berry and his
party when they made their unwise and impatient motion of want
of confidence without waiting for the Governor's speech.[2] He would
not willingly accept office alone, though prepared to go even that
length if his friends deemed it necessary and would agree to support
him, but felt sure that they would coincide with his opinion that he
should bring with him two colleagues, of whom one at least should

[2] Moved on 23 July 1880, although the Governor did not formally open Parliament
until 27 July. The Governor reproved the members of the Legislative Assembly for
having considered questions of public policy before the Crown or its representative had
formally opened Parliament.

have a portfolio. He was not then as definite as this, but I could gather from his remarks that this about represented his then opinion. From his house I went to Berry's where I explained Wrixon's views and discussed the situation. He had sent for me and sought my advice two days before so that this was not the first time I had proposed it to him. I found him still only too anxious to link himself with more distinguished associates, but at the same time harassed by the Catholic influences brought to bear by O'Shanassy and O'Loghlen and also that of the ultras of his party who made it plain that they intended to break away from him at once if he introduced any moderating element. Wrixon was to give his answer on the Monday (August 2 [1880]) and when he did so it was a courteous refusal. The *Argus* had employed every artifice to foment discord and prevent the coalition and it succeeded in postponing it for three years to the great loss and discredit of the colony. Then followed the interview with O'Shanassy in which he paved the way for his abandonment at the subsequent Opposition Caucus of his request for a Ministerial Commission upon the Education question, but insisted upon his demand for a place in the Cabinet equal to that of Berry and the nomination of two colleagues in addition to O'Loghlen.

At this Caucus and at that which had preceded it a week before I opposed any concession to the Catholics and when the meeting was over was one of the few whom Berry invited to accompany him to the White Hart Hotel[3] where he proceeded to make up his Ministry. He sent for me to the room to tell me that O'Loghlen had refused the Attorney-Generalship unless the Catholic claims were in some way to receive attention. I at once suggested my room-mate Vale, but Berry had no liking for him and to my intense amazement said, 'Why not take the position yourself—I like you and can work with you.' This was a startling offer to a complete novice, as it was usually the second office in the Cabinet but he was evidently desperate, dispirited by Wrixon's refusal and anxious to have the suspense terminated. I declined without an instant's hesitation on the ground of my unfitness for the post and again urged him to accept Vale. He did so. Colonel Smith and Patterson arrived and I withdrew. In an hour or two afterwards the Ministry was formed, not on the whole abler than his former cabinet but decidedly more respectable. Vale, in spite of a venomous tongue, and Richardson despite a selfish temper, were

---

[3] At the corner of Bourke and Spring Streets, opposite Parliament House.

upright, total abstainers and church members. Langridge and A. T.
Clark were far more amiable than those they succeeded while the
whole tone of the Government was raised by the inclusion of Pearson.
The excuse was made that as he was Patterson's colleague they could
not be both allotted offices and he was merely made a member of the
Executive Council. As a matter of fact he had a far better claim to
such a position than Patterson and though less efficient as an administrator would have proved a far more loyal colleague. Seeing the
radical tide on the ebb, Patterson, who had been one of the most
violent in the time of violence trimmed his sails now in exactly the
opposite direction and commenced his new cruise by jockeying his
colleague out of a place in the Government in order to secure it
for himself.

An Oxford don in habit, manner and culture, slight in frame, deli-
cate in constitution, refined, sensitive and gentle in disposition,
Pearson was governed in politics as in private life by the high ideals
of great thinkers and the standards of honour natural to an English
gentleman. He possessed one of the richest minds, most distinguished
gifts of literary style and widest ranges of information of any man
whom I have ever met, and though too academic as a speaker to
become a popular orator, grew in course of time to be a most effective
debater as well as the most polished and finished speaker of our
Parliament. The only man who could be compared with him was
Mr Murray Smith, his contemporary at Oxford, who like most of
the laissez-faire Liberals had become in course of time a colonial
Conservative. Pearson's sympathies were so large and generous that
Liberalism with him was the expression of his idealistic aims for
the elevation of the race. Murray Smith on the other hand became
by force of circumstances steeped in commercialism and though
never very successful in his operations imbibed the current prejudices
and defended the selfishness of the average business man.

Physically stronger than Pearson, with a richer voice and less shrink-
ing presence, he was the master of a choice and elegant style of
speaking, following the best English models and breathing a fairness
and graciousness that were captivating though a little mannered
and sometimes affected. He was in truth at all times a strong and
sometimes a bitter party man, well-grounded in all the doctrines of
the Cobden Club and by instinct on the side of the classes. Withal
he was on every occasion a thoughtful and sometimes an emotional

speaker rising momentarily to eloquence of a chastened fervour and often with touches of humour. Genuinely literary in taste, he was well-read and yet a society man, as keen in his enjoyment of his reading as Pearson though by comparison an amateur in study and much narrower in range. He was as a rule much more effective in the House and out of it because lighter, more at ease and much more closely in touch with his party than Pearson ever was, but at the same time Pearson at his best surpassed him at times and with his pen was of course incomparably his superior. They were linked together in spite of themselves in the eye of the House by their common tastes and characteristics but personally were never friendly. Smith sneered at Pearson as an unpractical ideologist while Pearson retorted that Smith's achievements consisted in the utterance of 'commonplaces pared to a point and twisted to a barb'. They combined to elevate the tone of the Assembly, to raise its level of style and to infuse into its arid wastes of dull irrelevancies the saving graces of literature, style and courtesy.

By comparison with the Berry Cabinet of 1877-9 that of 1880 was respectable and hard working. In truth its majority was so narrow and it was so soon deserted by some of its least reputable followers that an uncertain tenure of office kept it close at work until its close. Conscientious as Vale and Richardson were in their private relations, they were by no means averse to postponing the settlement of the Reform issue so as to prolong their tenure of office; and when the Ministerial Bill was returned amended from the Council found their colleagues willing allies in their proposals to lay the Bill aside so as to continue the agitation and their lease of power. In this they were supported by the *Age* which had become determined to exact reprisals upon the Conservatives who had so foolishly rejected its proffers of a coalition. It was at this juncture that I felt bound to separate even from my chief Berry, my friend Pearson, and my employer and friend Mr Syme, and to take up a course of my own in opposition to all of them but consistent with that which I had adopted at the opening of the session. The country was suffering from the continuance of strife; the difference between the two schemes was not great; if the opportunity were lost it was more than likely owing to the melting away of the Ministerial following that we should secure no reform at all, for the electors were losing interest in the unduly prolonged struggle and were becoming absorbed in the better business which the prospects promised. To be true to our pledges, to maintain our party and to serve our constituents it was in my opinion essential that we should accept a reasonable settlement if one were proffered to us from the other side.

I was young and had remained contrary to most expectations almost silent since my entrance to the House, attending regularly and voting loyally with my party, so that I had sunk almost out of sight of the Whips and party managers when the expression of my resolution to act upon my own judgment once more concentrated attention upon me: the angry attention of my associates, the delighted attention of our opponents. The circumstances that ensued were such as to throw my action into the strongest relief and expose me for the time to the greatest trials in my first declaration of political independence—independence of my party, my leader and of the *Age*—and assertion of my own right and intention to act without regard to them or even to the Reform Leagues in my constituency, in what I believed to be the interests of the country. The issue was of the utmost importance to the country and at the time absolutely overshadowed every other question. It was of some considerable importance even to a legislative stripling like myself, a mere freshman in politics as the *Age* contemptuously styled me; and as an analysis of the situation may be fairly taken as typical of what were termed great crises in Victorian public affairs it may be profitable to examine it in some detail since the factors in operation are those whose combination and impact determined the course of events then and on all other similar occasions. Looking backward what has happened always tends to appear inevitable, but while the fortune of each day is trembling in the balance no such comfortable doctrine can be maintained by those engaged in the struggle. There are, of course, cases in which the march of circumstance is evidently irresistible. This was not one of them. It was touch and go for weeks whether we were to have any Reform Bill at all.

8

'LEADERS AT A BOUND'

The Passing of the Reform Bill, 1881

IT WOULD BE TO INDULGE in too great a refinement to attempt to explain the reasons which led all the individual members of the Assembly to wish that the Reform question were settled. The bulk of them, like the bulk of the electors, were willing to accept almost any settlement and would soon have agreed to abandon the agitation altogether even if entirely unsuccessful, at all events for a few years. The great body of the Ministerialists desired it because they were pledged to this particular matter more than any other. The great body of the Opposition desired it because they realized that the formation of the Cabinet had left a sufficient number of the followers of the Government prepared to desert it at the first excuse. L. L. Smith, a hanger-on of the Catholic party without any standing in the House or out of it, was able to reduce the Ministerial majority to five, including Wrixon, in a direct vote of want of confidence; and although his chiefs O'Shanassy and O'Loghlen voted with him there remained at least as many of their associates with the Government as could have put them out if the time and the leader had presented themselves. The Reform question once settled, the course would be left clear for an attack that could not fail, as this did, to secure even a reply from the Treasury Benches. It was merely a matter of terms as to the qualification of voters and representatives which separated the two Houses and the difference might readily have been arranged but for the personal interests and passions of a number of the leaders.

Berry was by this time so weary of the agitation and so conscious that its force was nearly spent, that although he saw clearly enough that his Ministry could not long survive a settlement, he was prepared to take the risk and rely upon popular gratitude to replace him before long. Most of his colleagues were content to be guided by him, Vale and Richardson being the chief exceptions. For them,

fond as they were of fighting, and bitter antagonists, a prolongation
of the contest meant not only a gratification of their dispositions
but a continuance in office. But for the determined stand taken
by the *Age* they would have insisted upon maintaining a campaign for a drastic Reform Bill from the outset. As it was, when
the paper raised the cry of 'No Surrender' they rejoiced and by
its assistance carried Berry along with them. He had personally
been opposed to the most important provisions in both his own
Reform Bills, in the first to the general application of the Plebiscite
(as the Referendum was then styled), and in the second to the
preservation of an elective Council. He was on sound ground in
contending that financial details could not be well submitted to a
popular vote and that a nominee Upper Chamber, under reasonable
conditions as to tenure of office, would be more likely to provide
just that combination of independence and pliancy required if a
bicameral constitution is to work smoothly and efficiently. The
doctrinairism of the *Age*, however, involved him in many difficulties
and encumbered his practical political influence to such an extent
that he had to surrender much against his will upon both points.
Under these circumstances it was but natural that he should be quite
willing to cast aside his second scheme of Reform when the *Age*
consented. In this as in other instances the paper was misled by
ignorance of public opinion and an overestimate of its own authority.

Mr David Syme was a commanding personality physically and
mentally, liable to fits of passionate resentment and indignation,
either at what he conceived to be public abuses or at any crossing
of his own imperious will. A student because the bent of his disposition was to enquire into all things, sober, cautious and a devotee
of the methods of science in all questions which he dealt with
himself and for which he accepted responsibility, he was in
regard to political and social problems purely a theorist, adopting
the mathematical modes of abstract reasoning current during the
French Revolution except upon the vital question of Free Trade
of which he was an early, an unwavering and a highly capable antagonist. His editor and chief adviser, Mr A. L. Windsor, was a man
of most uncommon mental energy and versatility. Though not a
university graduate he was more classically trained than Syme, far
quicker and more adaptable, more eloquent and if necessary sophisti-
cal, probably even better read and a far readier, more copious and

polished writer and speaker. His general attitude of mind was sceptical and he regarded politics as a field of expediency in which force and address were the most serviceable qualifications. He had many enthusiasms but they were all short-lived, a fine literary taste and style, and a rich endowment of humour, insight and original speculation. His life, however, was that of a solitary; he avoided as far as possible all intercourse with the world around him, knowing it only through and dealing with it only in print. He too was a doctrinaire, less rigid and less consistent than Syme, of a domineering but far less persistent temper. Both were ambitious, egotistic, sensitive and pertinacious in personal hostilities. Utterly unlike in appearance, manners, taste, talent and disposition, they were too much alike in these respects with the consequence that the paper was frequently far more virulent, variable and unfair than it ought to have been having regard to their ability and its influence. The main motive with Mr Syme was hatred and rivalry of the *Argus*, to run counter to whose policy was too often his only aim. It opposed a Coalition and he strongly favoured it and became ardent in his support of Berry because he endeavoured to carry it out. When the *Argus* prepared to arrange a compromise on the Reform Bill for which the *Age* had been labouring for weeks, he at once reversed its attitude and declared for open war. Windsor, perfectly indifferent as a rule to the course to be followed, fell in at once with the wishes of his principal; and hence the crisis in the Liberal Party which threatened at the last moment to destroy all the labours of months and the hopes of the people for a settlement of the long and costly effort to secure a reasonable Reform of the Constitution.

O'Shanassy was perfectly consistent in his attitude towards the Reform Bill and statesmanlike in his treatment of the Ministry which had not only refused his alliance but selected in place of O'Loghlen the one man, Vale, who was most personally and denominationally obnoxious to him. He had sacrificed his opportunity of being serviceable to his Church rather than forfeit the position as joint head of the Government to which he conceived himself fully entitled. That exhibited the weak side of his character. Had he been less egotistical he would have played a far greater part in politics and accomplished far more than he did. Had he been joint leader with anyone his colleague would have required all the self-abnegation of a Christian martyr if a relationship were to even

seem to be preserved which would only be a mockery, so far as he
was concerned, from the first hour. He was biding his time with
imperturbable implacability and splendid reserve. O'Loghlen, a far
weaker man, had refused the Attorney-Generalship out of loyalty
first to his Church and second to O'Shanassy. The appointment of
Vale was to him an insult. Richardson, a leading Orangeman, was
almost equally offensive. He [O'Loghlen] crossed the floor at the
first opportunity and harassed the Government, not so much in
the former character of ultra which he had preserved in Cabinet but
as a moderate, cultivating friendly feelings with the Conservatives
among whom he sat. His motive obviously was to settle Reform in
order to overturn the Cabinet, a policy of which O'Shanassy approved
but by which he was too large-minded to be governed in such a
great issue. The former colleagues of Berry and O'Loghlen who had
been omitted from the Ministry—Longmore and Woods, especially
the former—[were] only matched in their bitterness against the
government by the disappointed office seekers who had sought their
vacant places, L. L. Smith, Bowman, Mirams.[1] McKean and Tucker
were equally ready for either emergency. Longmore, Woods and
Mirams preferred to remain ultras and to censure Berry for making
terms with the Opposition, while the others as a rule followed
O'Loghlen's lead and assailed them for frowning upon overtures
for peace. But these parties far from assailing each other were united
in hostility to the Government whose life hung upon a thread.

The consequence of the meeting of all these conflicting elements
was that the situation as it developed was at a critical moment in
the hands of two men—Fincham and myself. He was an upright,
amiable, consistent Liberal who had become disgusted with the
antics of the ultras in the late and present Berry administrations and
had unconsciously drifted somewhat out of sympathy with his party
and into sympathy with Conservative ideas.[2] The vacillation of the

[1] A scribble in the MS. after 'Mirams' is difficult to decipher but the final intention
seems to have been to mark a dash at this point, Deakin's usual sign for the end of
a sentence. It is possible however that the sentence should end at 'places'.
[2] George Randall Fincham, about whom the standard reference books are silent,
has sometimes been confused with George Fincham, the head of a firm of organ-
builders well-known in Melbourne. G. R. Fincham (1830-1901) was born in Hamp-
shire and came to Australia in the mid-fifties. He became a leather-merchant at Ballarat,
importing the leather belts used for engines in gold-mining. After some unsuccessful
investing in gold-mines, he did very well from his shares in a gold-mine at Barry's
Reef. He was a Member of the Legislative Assembly for Ballarat West from 1874 to
1886, but never held Ministerial office. In his last years he lived in Melbourne. His

Government under conflicting influences, coupled with his dislike of Vale and Richardson, finally alienated him altogether and he became in sentiment though not in fact a member of the Opposition. He stood by all the moderate proposals and at the Caucus when 27 voted for the abandonment of the Bill and 8 against it he stepped forward with the statement that in a question so vital to the community he could not accept the vote of the Caucus as binding and must take an independent course. To the surprise of everyone I followed with a similar declaration of independence, for though my ideas were well known it was thought my relation with the *Age* would have fettered my action. I think Bolton was present and indicated his intention to follow our lead, but as he was one of O'Shanassy's staunchest Catholics and already practically in Opposition, little heed was paid to him.

The grounds upon which Fincham and myself, who had up to this time seen little of each other, now prepared for joint action were the assurances we had received from the Opposition that though the *Argus* had announced the Council's last amendments as final and asserted that they would not be modified in any particular, the Council would under pressure concede two of our demands and meet us to a certain extent on the third.[3] Fincham put this to the Caucus very lamely for he was at no time a good speaker and was extremely nervous. For my part I said as little as possible except to announce my resolution, because I was confident that it would be unwise to pledge myself for the action of others and in the last resort was prepared to meet even a less advance than that outlined. The effect of our joint protest was decisive, for no such breakaway had occurred for many years, and the opposite sides [in the House] were so evenly balanced that it was known a vote or two would turn the decision

---

grandson, Mr R. W. Fincham of Ferny Creek, who has kindly supplied most of this information, recalls the family impression that he was 'too outspoken, and refused to toe the party line'.

[3] The two demands the Council were prepared to concede were that the proposed property qualification for members of the Council should be reduced from £150 to £100, and that the proposal that governments should necessarily include two Ministers from the Council should be abandoned. There were two other points still at issue: whether there should be higher rate-paying qualifications for leasehold as compared with freehold electors; and whether elections for all provinces should be held on the same day, so as to minimize plural voting in respect of property holdings in different electorates. Deakin's third demand here refers to the question of electors' qualifications. In the event the Council did not yield on this point, but did consent to the holding of all elections on the same day.

either way.[4] The Caucus broke up in confusion. We were treated as Ishmaelites. The majority of our colleagues drew away from us and we went out alone almost as melancholy as, according to Milton, Adam and Eve took their way from Eden after their expulsion.

I had come to my resolution quite independently of anyone in or out of Parliament, and felt my position the more critical because I was bound to be associated for the moment with men like Bolton who was already allied with the Opposition and with others like Fincham who were obviously tending that way. Of course I was being flattered by Murray Smith, then leader of the Opposition, who called at my private house to assure me that the Council would be coaxed into concessions; and by Ramsay, whose aim was a coalition in which Liberal Conservatives like Francis should join hands with the less aggressive men of our party. I was, however, equally determined that it was my duty to get the Reform crisis concluded and to preserve the Berry Ministry as the best available Liberal administration. More interviews followed in the little room off the Library where so many plots have been hatched, and where Fincham and I received from Murray Smith in his own writing a statement of the further concessions promised on behalf of the Council. These we took to the Ministerial rooms to Berry, who with Patterson and Langridge was willing to accept the overtures had not Vale and Richardson dissuaded him at a rather stormy interview from which Fincham withdrew rather abruptly, and in which Vale stigmatized us both as 'Wreckers', implying that we hoped for personal gain from the overthrow of the Ministry. Berry's final reply was that the proffer must be made publicly on the floor of the House and by a responsible member of the Opposition. Fincham did not, I think, press for this but I insisted upon it as essential. Ramsay, who chafed somewhat at Murray Smith's leadership and who was eager to associate himself with the settlement, when he saw Smith hesitate as he was accustomed to do in all emergencies, without waiting for permission sprang into the breach and gave the required assurance; largely, if I recollect aright, because I had insisted on it as the condition of my vote. Fincham was ready without it but this left 41 votes on each side. Ramsay's speech meant my adherence, giving an effective 42 for

4 This sentence is a conflation of two sentences in the MS. In expressing himself in an alternative way Deakin omitted to cancel his first version.

another Conference with the Council while at most only 40 could be counted upon to vote against it.

The dice were cast. The Bill was saved. After an anxious ten days, and two days in which I had lived as an exile with political extinction freely threatened, on strained relations with Berry to whom I was attached and with his colleagues with whom I was friendly, terms were arranged, a Conference held and the concessions promised us were obtained [16 June 1881]. Our action had saved the situation and secured the Bill.[5] Then from outcasts we became leaders at a bound. Fincham and I were publicly thanked in the House, though so were some men prepared to cross over on any pretext.[6] The *Age* and the Ministry claimed a victory. My vote had been the last and perhaps least, but most decisive factor in this all important achievement.

What would have happened if I had not fought for the Conference at the risk of expulsion from the party and loss of my seat it is of course impossible to say. Given the antagonism of Fincham, the ultras and the Catholics to the Ministry the most probable effect would have been to detach one or two of the dissentient Ministerialists, defeat the Government and bring in a new Reform Bill which could not have been carried against the Liberal opposition of Berry and the *Age*. The whole course of events would in any case have been different. It is even possible that the Ministry might have promulgated an extreme policy and lived a little longer upon it. It is most probable that the Reform Bill would have been lost. The curious concatenation of circumstances, intrigues, personal aims and faction cross currents by which it was carried serve at least to illustrate the extreme complexity of every important political crisis and the curiously confused and intricate tangle of events and relations which go to make up its course and conditions from day to day.

That I am not exaggerating my own part in this, or at all events

[5] The main provisions were a reduction of the tenure of the Legislative Councillors from ten to six years, an increase in the number of members from thirty to forty-two, an extention of the franchise and a lowering of the property qualification of members. The power of the Council did not in fact decline, but head-on collisions with the Assembly were avoided for many years.

[6] See *Victoria, Parliamentary Debates*, vol. xxxvi. O'Loghlen, for example, said in a post-mortem debate after the issue was settled: 'He would take this opportunity of paying a tribute to the manliness and firmness of the honourable member for Ballarat West (Mr Fincham), who was one of the main agents in bringing about a settlement of the reform question. Two other honourable members also deserved credit in connection with the matter—his honourable colleague (Mr Deakin) and the honourable member for Moira (Mr Bolton). Both these honourable members manfully spoke out their convictions' (p. 2751).

my singularity, was made plain immediately after by the vote of want
of confidence moved by O'Loghlen when Fincham and Bolton openly
joined the Opposition, and when Longmore, Mirams and Tucker
only voted for the Ministry under the whip while privately and
publicly assailing them all they dared. Of all who had resisted them
in regard to the Reform Bill I was the only one who supported them
strongly in their hour of trial. The result of the division disillusioned
me.[7] I had accepted, as expressing their true sentiments and rule of
practice, the protests of Murray Smith, Francis, Kerferd, Gillies,
Ramsay and others against mere party ends and party action in
defiance of personal judgment and conscience—[protests made] while
they were seeking to win votes from the majority.[8] I found them
dragged at the tail of their own less scrupulous followers as shame-
lessly as the Government had been during its recent vacillations.
There was not a pin to choose between them and I despised them
both, though the course of the next eighteen months witnessed a
degradation of the Conservatives more pitiable and less honourable
than anything Berry or his party had ever endured.

Murray Smith and his chief associates, with the single exception
of Wrixon whose conduct throughout was that of an honourable,
high-minded and public-spirited statesman, conceded to their greedy
and revengeful rank and file the support necessary to turn out the
Government but at the same time entered into a compact with one
another to decline to join him [Wrixon]. Their expectation was that
he would be unable to form a Ministry and that Murray Smith would
be sent for, and Sir Bryan having been provided for, a Cabinet
constructed in which probably Francis would take the lead, reinforc-
ing his old regiment of 1874-5 with a few new men. The Berry
Ministry fell, having a majority of three against them, and so far
their expectations were realized. But they little knew the breezy
self-confidence of O'Loghlen, particularly when acting under the
advice of Bent, the most brazen, untrustworthy . . . intriguer
whom the Victorian Assembly had ever known. The leaders of
the party having stood aside, he promptly filled their places with
new and untried men of the most mediocre capacity. He himself
had less than three years' Parliamentary experience, half that term

7 The Berry Government was defeated on O'Loghlen's motion of want of confidence
by 41 votes to 38, on 30 July 1881.
8 The sentence in the MS. has here been slightly re-arranged.

spent in office.[9] Grant it is true was a veteran, but then in his decay. Bent had been six months Minister of Public Works but all the rest were novices. Burrowes and Young had held their seats for years among the silent inconsiderable section of the steady Conservative rank and file. Graves, much younger in politics, was their senior in age and the most sinuous and uncertain of rail-sitters. Bolton had been eighteen months a Member, notable for nothing but for having in that time twice changed sides. Gaunson, with more than twice the experience, was even flightier and having received the Chairmanship of Committees from Mr Berry turned upon him treacherously within the year for the promise of a higher post. Endowed with a musical voice, good presence, fine flow of language, great quickness of mind, readiness of retort and a good deal of industry, ability and humour he was only disqualified from marked successes by his utter instability, egregious egotism, want of consistency and violence of temper. L. L. Smith . . . accepted a portfolio without office as he dared not face his constituents, while Fincham who was equally cowed though willing to take office declined the barren compliment. Strange to say, a stolid, sturdy, honourable old Tory in the Council, Sir James MacBain, was less particular; and when Gaunson was defeated in endeavouring to regain his seat as a Minister, Mr Walter Madden, one of the ablest and most upright young Conservatives, accepted the vacancy. Still never was there such a scratch team constituted in Victoria. Its downfall within a few weeks was considered inevitable and it was only composed at last in desperation and defiance of the Opposition from whom it sprang. Several minor members like Zox declined to join them, for though eager to attain Cabinet rank the tenure was too ridiculously insecure to tempt even them. It was really a Bent Ministry at last, for it was he who cajoled MacBain, Young and Burrowes into lending it a strain of respectability; while L. L. Smith and Graves were men after his own heart. . . .

He was a kind of sober Falstaff in appearance, bonhomie, cheeriness and absence of moral or any other principle. A rare manager of men, cunning, resourceful, specious, voluble and of inexhaustible impudence he had become a master of the craft of snaring them.

---

[9] O'Loghlen had arrived in Australia in 1862 and practised at the bar. He succeeded to a baronetcy in 1877, and was elected to the Assembly at a by-election in January 1878. He was Attorney-General from March 1878 to March 1880.

. . . How colleagues as estimable as O'Loghlen, Grant, MacBain and Madden came to submit to such an associate it is hard to say, but they did. It was he who constituted, controlled and preserved the Ministry.

My action in regard to them was not dictated by any personal motive. Bent had indirectly suggested that office was open to me, as he probably had suggested it to a score of others without any intention beyond that of trapping a vote, but O'Loghlen made overtures in his gentlemanly awkward way that I at once disposed of without any qualification. His motive was not altogether as rash as might appear since he realized how unsafe his seat for West Bourke was without my aid. He told me frankly afterwards that his object had been that we should have gone to the constituency together as colleagues. He was only returned as it proved by 60 votes against a weak opponent, in a contest in which I took no part whatever, being in Sydney at the time.[10] It was on my way thither that I met O'Shanassy in the dining room, I think at Junee, gulping down his food in his customary rough way. He was so consumed with rage that he could not contain himself and even to me burst out into a complaint of his wrongs which was intense in its bitterness and fury. It was in truth the close of his career that I was witnessing without knowing it, and that he was realizing. His reflections must naturally have been inflamed and wrathful like his speech. He had helped to strike down the Berry Government and had found his services unrecognized and almost scorned by the Conservatives. He had then helped to strike down the Service Government and, intoxicated with success, had allowed his egotism and ambition to destroy the one opportunity of power presented in his later career, during the composition of the new Berry Government. He had then conducted a third campaign, labouring and biding his time and had finally with vengeful glee struck down the Liberal Ministry formed without him. He had accomplished this, fighting by the side and in the interest of his co-religionist and political ally who had refused office so recently, partly for his sake. The prize at last was within his grasp. The Premiership, at least in fact if not in name, and probably in both, was his and the attainment of his life's aims. But Bent had too well gauged the situation and Grant, the Nestor of the little group, con-

[10] 26 July 1881. On accepting office, Ministers were then required to re-submit themselves to the electors.

curred that such a selection would be fatal to the incoming team. 'O'Loghlen sent for me,' he said, his eyes blazing, his great form shaking and his deep voice rolling around the refreshment room to the amazement of the passengers: 'He sent for me as he was obliged to and offered me . . . offered *me* . . . '—this almost in a roar as he flung himself round in his chair, turning his back upon me as he concluded speechless with indignation, mortification and despair yet with a fine ring of courageous contemptuous satire under all—'He offered me—a seat directly behind him!' And so the old lion, his prey escaped, returned for the last time to his den.

[Here the MS. concludes. It is followed by a page headed 'P.S.', initialled by Deakin and dated 4 December 1900.]

The remainder of these articles must wait. The formation of the first coalition [1883] and its inner history. Of the second [1886] and its several enterprises. The inclusion of Patterson and the audacity with which he posed as the man responsible for calling out the troops [August 1890, during the shipping strike], with which he had nothing whatever to do as it was decided by Gillies, Bell and myself and he had nothing to say to it even in Cabinet, except to endorse it. The fall of the Ministry [November 1890]. My resolution to devote myself to the creation of an independent position in the House without accepting office, and to the Federal cause. How I helped to defeat the Shiels Government [1892-3] and more than anyone did defeat the Patterson Government [1893-4], and made and sustained that of Turner [1894-9].

G

APPENDIX A

PERSONS MENTIONED IN THE TEXT

In these brief notes all appointments, offices held, etc., refer to Victoria unless otherwise stated. The description of occupation when available, is in many cases necessarily inexact, especially for those in 'business' of some kind. For politicians the year of first entry to the Legislative Assembly is given, e.g., M.L.A. 1863, but later intervals when the subject was not in Parliament are not recorded. In most cases the titles of Ministerial offices held have not been given in detail; there were often changes within the lifetime of a single government.

The standard sources have been used, e.g., P. Serle, *Dictionary of Australian Biography* (Sydney, 1949); the various biographical compilations of Fred Johns; P. Mennell, *Dictionary of Australasian Biography* (London, 1892); A. Sutherland, *Victoria and its Metropolis* (Melbourne, 1888); H. M. Humphreys, *Men of the Time* (Melbourne, 1882); and others. In addition many details have been uncovered by Miss M. Kiddle, and by Mr P. Garrett and the research staff of the Public Library of Victoria.

BELL, James (1836-1908); arrived in Victoria 1857; grain and coal merchant; member Legislative Council 1882; held Ministerial office 1886, 1889.

BENT, (Sir) Thomas (1838-1909); b. New South Wales; arrived in Melbourne 1849; market gardener; M.L.A. 1871; held Ministerial office 1880, 1881, 1902; Speaker 1892; Premier 1904-8; knighted 1908.

BERRY, (Sir) Graham (1822-1904); b. England; arrived in Victoria 1852; shopkeeper and journalist; M.L.A. 1860; Treasurer 1870; Premier 1875, 1877-80, 1880-1; Chief Secretary in coalition government with James Service, 1883-6; Treasurer 1892-3; Speaker 1894-7; knighted 1886.

BOLTON, Henry (1842-1900); b. Ireland; arrived in Victoria 1861; brewer; M.L.A. 1880; Postmaster-General 1881; later went to Queensland.

BOWEN, (Sir) George Ferguson (1821-99); b. Ireland; chief secretary of government in Ionian Islands 1854; governor of Queensland 1859, of New Zealand 1868, of Victoria 1873, of Mauritius 1879, of Hong Kong 1882; knighted 1856; P.C. 1886.

BOWMAN, Robert (?-1893); M.L.A. 1866-71, 1877-86, 1889-93.

BURROWES, Robert (1827-93); b. Canada; arrived in Victoria 1853; mining interests; M.L.A. 1866; Minister of Mines 1881.

CAMERON, Donald (1841-88); journalist; M.L.A. for West Bourke 1877.

CASEY, James Joseph (1831-1913); b. Ireland; arrived in Victoria 1855; country newspaper proprietor; M.L.A. 1861; called to bar 1865; held Ministerial office 1868-9, 1872-5; county court judge 1884.

CLARK, Alfred Thomas (1845-88); b. England; arrived in Victoria 1852; auctioneering business and newspaper proprietor; M.L.A. 1871; held Ministerial office 1880.

DEAKIN, Alfred (1856-1919); b. Victoria; barrister and journalist; M.L.A. 1879; commissioner of public works and water supply 1883; Chief Secretary 1886-90; delegate to Colonial conference 1887; worked for federation 1890-1900; Attorney-General of the Commonwealth 1901; Prime Minister 1903-4, 1905-8, 1909-10.

DUFFY, (Sir) Charles Gavan (1816-1903); b. Ireland; prominent in the Irish nationalist movement as editor of the *Nation*; M.P. 1850; emigrated to Victoria 1855; M.L.A. 1856; held Ministerial office 1857, 1858, 1861; Premier 1871-2; Speaker 1877-80; returned to Europe 1880; knighted 1873.

DUFFY, John Gavan (1844-1917); b. Ireland; son of (Sir) Charles Gavan Duffy; arrived in Victoria 1859; barrister; M.L.A. 1874; held Ministerial office 1880, 1890, 1894.

FINCHAM, George Randall (1830-1901); b. England; arrived in Australia c. 1855; leather merchant and mining interests; M.L.A. 1874. See p. 74.

FRANCIS, James Goodall (1819-84); b. England; arrived in Tasmania 1834, Victoria 1853; merchant; M.L.A. 1859; held Ministerial office 1859, 1863, 1870; Premier 1872-4.

GAUNSON, David (1846-1909); b. New South Wales; came to Victoria as a child; solicitor; M.L.A. 1875; Minister in O'Loghlen ministry 1881, but defeated on presenting for re-election.

GILLIES, Duncan (1834-1903); b. Scotland; arrived in Victoria 1852; miner; M.L.A. 1859; held Ministerial office 1872, 1875, 1880, 1883; Premier 1886-90; Agent-General for Victoria 1894; re-entered Legislative Assembly 1897; Speaker 1902.

GRANT, James Macpherson (1822-85); b. Scotland; arrived Sydney 1836, Victoria 1853; solicitor; M.L.A. 1856; held Ministerial office 1861, 1863, 1871, 1877, 1881; best known in connection with his Land Acts, 1865 and 1869.

GRAVES, James Howlin (1827-?); b. Ireland; arrived in Victoria 1864; pastoral business; M.L.A. 1877; held Ministerial office 1881; Chairman of Committees 1903-4.

HARPER, Robert (1842-1919); b. Scotland; arrived in Victoria 1856; merchant; M.L.A. 1879; member of the House of Representatives 1901.

HIGINBOTHAM, George (1826-92); b. Ireland; arrived in Victoria 1854; journalist and barrister; M.L.A. 1861; Attorney-General 1863; retired from politics 1876; judge of Supreme Court 1880; Chief Justice 1886; a famous orator and Liberal leader.

KERFERD, George Briscoe (1831-89); b. England; arrived in Victoria 1853; barrister; M.L.A. 1864; held Ministerial office 1868, 1872, 1875, 1880, 1883; Premier 1874-5; judge of Supreme Court 1885.

LALOR, Peter (1827-89); b. Ireland; arrived in Victoria 1852; engineer; a leader of the diggers at the Eureka stockade 1854; M.L.A. 1856; held Ministerial office 1875, 1877; Speaker 1880-7.

LANGRIDGE, George David (1829-91); b. England; arrived in Victoria 1852; builder; held Ministerial office 1880, 1883, 1890.

LONGMORE, Francis (1826-98); b. Ireland; arrived Sydney 1839, Victoria 1852; farmer; M.L.A. 1864; held Ministerial office 1871, 1875, 1877.

MacBAIN, (Sir) James (1828-92); b. Scotland, arrived in Victoria 1853; commercial and pastoral pursuits; M.L.A. 1864; member Legislative Council 1880; Minister without portfolio 1881; knighted 1886.

McCULLOCH, (Sir) James (1819-93); b. Scotland; arrived in Victoria 1853; merchant; member of old Legislative Council 1854; M.L.A. 1856; Premier 1863-8, 1868-9, 1870-1, 1875-7; knighted 1870.

McKEAN, James (1832-1901); b. Ireland; arrived in Victoria c. 1854; journalist and solicitor; M.L.A. 1865; Minister for Lands September 1869-April 1870.

MacMAHON, (Sir) Charles (1824-91); b. Ireland; arrived in Victoria 1852; soldier and Commissioner of Police, resigned 1858; M.L.A. 1861; Speaker 1871-7, 1880; knighted 1875.

MADDEN, Walter (1848-1925); b. Ireland; arrived in Victoria 1857; surveyor; M.L.A. 1880; Minister for Lands 1881.

MICHIE, (Sir) Archibald (1813-99); b. England; arrived New South Wales 1839, Victoria 1852; barrister and journalist; M.L.A. 1856; held Ministerial office 1857, 1863, 1870; Agent-General for Victoria 1873-9; knighted 1878.

MIRAMS, James (1839-1916); b. England; arrived in Victoria 1857; secretary of building society; M.L.A. 1874.

MUNRO, James (1832-1908); b. Scotland; arrived in Victoria 1858; founded Victorian Permanent Building Society 1865; M.L.A. 1874; Premier November 1890-February 1892.

O'LOGHLEN, (Sir) Bryan (1828-1905); b. Ireland; arrived in Victoria 1862; barrister; M.L.A. 1877; succeeded to baronetcy 1877; Attorney-General 1878; Premier 1881-3.

O'SHANASSY, (Sir) John (1818-83); b. Ireland; arrived in Victoria 1839; farmer, shopkeeper; M.L.A. 1856; Premier for short periods 1857, 1858; Premier 1861-3; member Legislative Council 1867; re-entered Legislative Assembly 1877; knighted 1874.

PARKES, (Sir) Henry (1815-96); b. England; arrived in New South Wales 1839; editor of *Empire* 1850-8; in politics from 1850's; Colonial Secretary 1866, and from then the most prominent figure in the politics of New South Wales, five times Premier; knighted 1877.

PATTERSON, (Sir) James Brown (1833-95); b. England; arrived in Victoria 1852; farmer; M.L.A. 1870; held Ministerial office 1875, 1877, 1880, 1889; Premier 1893-4; knighted 1894.

PEARSON, Charles Henry (1830-94); b. England; entered Oriel College, Oxford 1849; Professor of Modern History, King's College, London 1855; visited Australia 1864, returned 1871; Lecturer in History, University of Melbourne 1874; M.L.A. 1878; Minister of Public Instruction 1886; author of historical and literary works, and writer for the *Age*.

PURVES, James Liddell (1843-1910); b. Victoria; called to English bar 1865; returned to Victoria 1866; barrister; M.L.A. 1872; a leader in Australian Natives' Association.

RAMSAY, Robert (1842-82); b. Scotland; arrived in Victoria 1847; solicitor; M.L.A. 1870; held Ministerial office 1872, 1874, 1875, 1880.

REID, (Sir) George Houston (1845-1918); b. Scotland; arrived in Australia 1852; barrister; Premier of New South Wales 1894-9; Prime Minister 1904-5; Australian High Commissioner in London 1909-16; knighted 1909.

RICHARDSON, Richard (?-?); b. England; arrived in Victoria 1852; farmer; M.L.A. 1874-94; Minister for Lands 1880.

SERVICE, James (1823-99); b. Scotland; arrived in Victoria 1853; merchant; M.L.A. 1857; Treasurer 1874; Premier 1880, 1883-6; member Legislative Council 1888.

SHIELS, William (1849-1904); b. Ireland; arrived in Victoria c. 1853; barrister; M.L.A. 1880; held Ministerial office 1890, 1899, 1902; Premier, February 1892-January 1893.

SMITH, Louis Lawrence (1830-1910); b. England; arrived in Victoria c. 1852; medical practice and commercial interests; M.L.A. 1859; Minister without portfolio 1881.

SMITH, Robert Murray (1831-1921); b. England; entered Oriel College, Oxford 1849; arrived in Australia 1854; commercial pursuits; M.L.A. 1872; Agent-General 1882-6.

SMITH, William Collard (1830-94); b. England; arrived in Victoria 1852; mining interests in Ballarat; M.L.A. 1861; held Ministerial office 1875, 1877, 1880; prominent in Volunteer force.

STAUGHTON, Samuel Thomas (1837-1901); b. and educated England; barrister; M.L.A. 1880.

SYME, David (1827-1908); b. Scotland; arrived in Victoria 1852; journalist; with his brother Ebenezer (d. 1860) purchased the *Age* 1856; from 1860 controlled policy of the *Age*, and had powerful influence on Victorian politics; influential in advocacy of protection; published *Outlines of an Industrial Science*, critical of orthodox political economy, 1876.

SYME, George (1821-94); b. Scotland; joined staff of the *Age* 1862; editor of the *Leader* to 1885; brother of David Syme.

TUCKER, Albert Lee (1843-1902); b. Victoria; commercial pursuits; M.L.A. 1874; Minister for Lands 1886.

TURNER, (Sir) George (1851-1916); b. Victoria; solicitor; M.L.A. 1889; held Ministerial office 1891; Premier 1894-9, 1900; first Treasurer of the Commonwealth 1901-4, and 1904-5; retired from politics 1906; knighted 1897.

VALE, William Mountford Kinsey (c. 1832-95); newsagent and barrister; M.L.A. 1864; held Ministerial office 1866, 1868, 1871; Attorney-General 1880; resigned from Parliament 1881.

WILLIAMS, Henry Roberts (?-?); M.L.A. 1877-1902; held Ministerial office 1880, 1894.

WILLOUGHBY, Howard (1839-1908); b. England; arrived in Australia 1857; various newspaper positions; chief of staff of *Argus* 1885, editor 1898-1903.

WINDSOR, Arthur Lloyd (1836-1913); b. Barbados; came to Victoria c. 1860; on *Argus* and country newspapers; editor of *Age* 1872-1900; retired to England.

WOODS, John (1822-92); b. England; arrived in Victoria 1852; engineer; M.L.A. 1859; Minister for Railways 1875, 1877.

WRIXON, (Sir) Henry John (1839-1913); b. Ireland; arrived in Victoria 1850; called to Irish bar 1861; barrister in Victoria 1863; M.L.A. 1868; held Ministerial office 1870, 1886; member Legislative Council 1896; knighted 1892.

YOUNG, Charles (?-?); M.L.A. 1874-92; held Ministerial office 1881.

ZOX, Ephraim L. (c. 1840-99); came to Victoria c. 1850; merchant; a leader of Melbourne Jewish community; M.L.A. 1877.

APPENDIX B

DEAKIN'S FIRST ELECTION ADDRESS

To the Electors of West Bourke

Gentlemen,

I beg to offer myself as a candidate for the seat rendered vacant by the decease of your late member, Mr J. T. Smith, and as I believe my political views to be of the same complexion I trust to obtain the support you have so long granted to him.

The reform of the constitution has, in my opinion, become an absolute necessity, arising out of our national growth. The scheme introduced by the Ministry last session would, I believe, effectually prevent the recurrence of deadlocks, and it has accordingly my cordial support. The objections taken to the plebiscite appear to me to be equally applicable to universal suffrage, and I do not see, therefore, how any really Liberal politician can entertain them for a single moment. It not only solves the problem of finality, but it has the additional recommendation of being a useful educational agent.

The subject of land legislation is of scarcely inferior importance, and seems to me in fact to be indissolubly bound up with the reform question. Whilst the territorial interest continues to have such dominant power as it possesses under our present constitution, experience shows it is idle to agitate for a land law that would place population on the land instead of cattle and sheep. A tax upon land is one of the instruments which can be effectually employed for this purpose; and while I would be no party to imposing an unfair burden upon any class, I should have no hesitation about correcting the irregularities of the present system where investigation has shown it to be necessary.

Of the Education Act I feel myself compelled to speak in no doubtful tones. I would resist any attempt whatever, from whatever quarter it might come, to introduce denominationalism into the State School, satisfied, as I am, that religious instruction can best be imparted by the religious instructor outside.

Protection is the only other subject on which a Liberal candidate, addressing a Liberal electorate is called upon to express his views. As Free-trade, practically, reduces itself, in a community like this, to commercial economy, I do not see how any Liberal, to be consistent, can be a Free-trader. Just as the object of our land legislation should be to promote the agricultural industry, so it should be the aim of our fiscal policy to provide employment for the mechanic and artisan. The revision of the tariff will form part of the business of next session, and in any

87

readjustment of the duties that may take place, all efforts should be directed to protect the interests of local labour against foreign competition.

On other matters of inferior concern I hope to be able to explain my views fully and unreservedly in person.

ALFRED DEAKIN.

[The *Age*, 8 February 1879. Written, according to Deakin (p. 26 above) at the dictation of A. L. Windsor, editor of the *Age*.]

APPENDIX C

VICTORIAN MINISTRIES, 1877-83

BERRY MINISTRY

Assumed office, 21 May 1877; Retired, 5 March 1880

Graham Berry	Premier and Chief Secretary
do	Treasurer
succeeded by	
William Collard Smith	do (*without salary*)
succeeded by	
Graham Berry	do
Francis Longmore	President of the Board of Land and Works, Commissioner of Crown Lands and Survey Minister of Agriculture
William Collard Smith	Minister of Mines, Minister of Public Instruction
James Brown Patterson	Commissioner of Public Works, Vice-President of the Board of Land and Works
Robert LePoer Trench	Attorney-General
succeeded by	
Sir Bryan O'Loghlen, Bt.	do
James Macpherson Grant	Minister of Justice
Peter Lalor	Commissioner of Trade and Customs
John Woods	Commissioner of Railways and Roads, Vice-President of the Board of Land and Works
Peter Lalor	Postmaster-General
succeeded by	
Henry Cuthbert, M.L.C.	do
succeeded by	
James Brown Patterson	do (*without salary*)

SERVICE MINISTRY

Assumed office, 5 March 1880; Retired, 3 August 1880

James Service	Premier and Treasurer
Robert Ramsay	Chief Secretary
George Briscoe Kerferd	Attorney-General
John Madden	Minister of Justice

Duncan Gillies	Commissioner of Railways
John Gavan Duffy	President of the Board of Land and Works, Commissioner of Crown Lands and Survey
Thomas Bent	Commissioner of Public Works
Robert Clark	Minister of Mines
Henry Cuthbert, M.L.C.	Commissioner of Trade and Customs
Robert Ramsay	Minister of Education (*without salary*)
Henry Cuthbert, M.L.C.	Postmaster-General (*without salary*)
James Goodall Francis	(*without office*)
Robert Stirling Anderson, M.L.C.	(*without office*)
Duncan Gillies	Vice-President of the Board of Land and Works (*without salary*)
Thomas Bent	Vice-President of the Board of Land and Works (*without salary*)
John Gavan Duffy	Minister of Agriculture (*without salary*)
Robert Clark	Commissioner of Water Supply (*without salary*)

BERRY MINISTRY

Assumed office, 3 August 1880; Retired, 9 July 1881

Graham Berry	Premier, Chief Secretary, Treasurer
William Mountford Kinsey Vale	Attorney-General, Minister of Justice
Richard Richardson	President of the Board of Land and Works, Commissioner of Crown Lands and Survey
James Brown Patterson	Commissioner of Railways
William Collard Smith	Minister of Education
Alfred Thomas Clark	Commissioner of Trade and Customs
Henry Roberts Williams	Minister of Mines
George David Langridge	Commissioner of Public Works
Richard Richardson	Minister of Agriculture (*without salary*)
George David Langridge	Vice-President of the Board of Land and Works (*without salary*)
James Brown Patterson	Vice-President of the Board of Land and Works (*without salary*)
Charles Henry Pearson	(*without office*)
Robert Dyce Reid	(*without office*)

O'LOGHLEN MINISTRY

Assumed office, 9 July 1881; Retired, 8 March 1883

Sir Bryan O'Loghlen, Bt.   Premier and Attorney-General
James Macpherson Grant   Chief Secretary
Thomas Bent   Commissioner of Railways
Frank Stanley Dobson, M.L.C.   Solicitor-General
James Howlin Graves   Commissioner of Trade and Customs

Charles Young   Minister of Water Supply and Agriculture

Henry Bolton   Postmaster-General
David Gaunson   President of the Board of Land and Works, Commissioner of Crown Lands and Survey

succeeded by
Walter Madden   do
Sir Bryan O'Loghlen, Bt.   Treasurer (*without salary*)
James Macpherson Grant   Minister of Public Instruction (*without salary*)

Thomas Bent   Vice-President of the Board of Land and Works (*without salary*)

Charles Young   Minister of Mines (*without salary*)
succeeded by
Robert Burrowes   do
Charles Young   Commissioner of Public Works, Vice-President of the Board of Land and Works (*without salary*)

Louis Lawrence Smith   (*without office*)
James MacBain, M.L.C.   (*without office*)

INDEX

References to persons are only to those prominent in the narrative and to passages where they are mentioned in detail. See also Appendix A.

Age newspaper, 4, 6, 46, 52, 61, 69, 70, 72, 73, 77
Argus newspaper, 3, 5, 6, 46, 61, 67, 73, 75

Barry's Reef, dramatic incident at, 50-1
Bent, Sir Thomas, 78-9
Berry, Sir Graham, early career, 13, 14; rise to power, 14; personal characteristics, 14, 22; moderation, 20; return from 'embassy' (1879), 21; appearance, 21-2; confidence in Deakin, 63, 67; difficulties over Reform Bills, 71-2
'Black Wednesday' (1878), 17
Bowen, Sir George, conduct in crisis, 19-20

Cameron, Donald, 40
Catholic vote, 12, 43, 57, 65
Conservative party, xiii, 11-12

Deakin, Alfred, writes *Victorian Politics* (1900) xi; on political history, 1, 2, 61; schooldays, 2; connection with *Age*, 5; views on free trade, 6; candidate for West Bourke (1879), 10; first political speech, 26-7; first elected to Parliament, 34; moves Address in Reply and resigns, 41-2; loses second election, 43; loses third election, 54; established as public speaker, 55; wins fourth election, 57; youthful aspirations, 58-60; views on coalitions, 62; decides to take independent action on

Reform Bill, 69-70; negotiates compromise, 76-7

Education Act (1872), 12n., 27, 45

Fincham, G. R., acts with Deakin on Reform Bill, 74-5

Grant, J. M., 15
'Greenbacks', rumoured issue of, 18

Harper, Robert, 24
Higinbotham, George, 22

Lalor, Peter, 15, 17
Liberal party, xiii, 12
Longmore, Francis, 15, 16

Newham, consequence of incomplete poll at, 35-8

O'Loghlen, Sir Bryan, 15, 63
O'Shanassy, Sir John, 63-4; rage at omission from O'Loghlen ministry, 80-1

Parnaby, Joyce E., xi, xv, 9, 18n.
Patterson, J. B., 15, 27, 30
Pearson, C. H., 3-4, 68-9

Reform Bill (1881), differences between Assembly and Council, 71, 75n.
Reform Leagues, 9n.
Rusden, G. W., bias of his *History*, xii, 61

Service, James, 12, 15, 56
Smith, R. Murray, 68-9

Smith, W. Collard, 15, 16
Syme, David, 6-7, 72-3

Turner, Henry Gyles, bias of his
   History, xii

Vale, W. M. K., 7-8

West Bourke electorate 1879, 8
Woods, John, 15, 33-4
Windsor, A. L., 26, 72-3
Wrixon, Sir Henry, 65-7